S0-AUO-314

LIFE
AND
DEATH
IN ONE
BREATH

SADHGURU
Yogi, Mystic and Visionary

JAICO PUBLISHING HOUSE

Ahmedabad Bangalore Bhopal Bhubaneswar Chennai
Delhi Hyderabad Kolkata Lucknow Mumbai

Published by Jaico Publishing House
A-2 Jash Chambers, 7-A Sir Phirozshah Mehta Road
Fort, Mumbai - 400 001
jaicopub@jaicobooks.com
www.jaicobooks.com

© Isha Foundation

To be sold only in India, Bangladesh, Bhutan,
Pakistan, Nepal, Sri Lanka and the Maldives.

LIFE AND DEATH IN ONE BREATH
ISBN 978-81-8495-442-5

First Jaico Impression: 2013
Fifteenth Jaico Impression: 2017

No part of this book may be reproduced or utilized in
any form or by any means, electronic or
mechanical including photocopying, recording or by any
information storage and retrieval system,
without permission in writing from the publishers.

Printed by
SRK Graphics
F-6, Gali No. 4A,
Friends Colony Industrial Ares, Delhi - 95

Sadhguru

CONTENTS

Sadhguru

INTRODUCTION

From time immemorial, people's lives have been punctuated with celebrations. From the first walking steps to the first job, from weddings and anniversaries to birthdays and baby showers, cultures around the world welcome the milestones of life with enthusiastic festivity. Every culture has evolved detailed customs and traditions for various stages of life to help one live in the best way possible. However, when it comes to the end of life, our celebratory spirits are faced with a dead end.

While the rituals of our lives are the outcome of generations of life experience, passed on from our predecessors, the rituals pertaining to death tend to spring from our belief rather than understanding – simply because there is no one to share that experience with us. Our ignorance renders us ill equipped to truly assist one who has stepped beyond our borders into the unknown. Furthermore, in trying to escape the fear that results from our ignorance, we have developed a prevalent attitude that death happens only to other people, not to us. When it comes to one's own death, no one seems to look forward to it, much less celebrate it. We are prejudiced: favoring life and fearing death, because of which we unknowingly create an irreconcilable gulf between the two.

Sadhguru reveals how this preference for life over death is self-defeating; paradoxical as it may seem, in trying to avoid death, we end up avoiding life itself. A constant underlying fear of death only prevents us from experiencing life to the fullest. He points out that life and death are inseparable. Only one who understands this, who is willing to accept the reality of death wholeheartedly, can ever hope to live totally. Conversely, only one who has lived fully will be prepared to die gracefully.

Having mastered the mechanisms of life at both ends of this existential spectrum, Sadhguru tells us how we can prepare for death and, in the process, plunge into the depths of life. He not only addresses the inevitability of death but also goes into the very nature of this inexplicable phenomenon. Going into the specifics, he describes what exactly happens to the body and mind during death. Proceeding even further, he talks about the true meaning of heaven and hell and uncovers the deep connection between spirituality and mortality.

He says the potent spiritual possibility that death presents is something all of us can make use of. Sadhguru urges even those who have lived a life devoid of spiritual processes, not to waste the valuable opportunity that unfolds as one transits into the non-physical realm. Lastly, not one to leave the matter incomplete, he conveys how to assist others during, and even after, the critical moment of passage, so that we can do something for them that perhaps, they could not do for themselves.

Compiled here are a collection of discourses by Sadhguru on various aspects of life and death. Starting with everyday life situations, including love, relationships and management, he delves into the core of human suffering and longing. Then, cutting through the hurdles of limited identities, values and beliefs, he shows the way to boundless inclusiveness. As we read the pages, and the chains of our bondage become clearer, he speaks of the importance of seeking help – and offers it to us.

Drawing from an ocean of knowing, Sadhguru is a rare mystic of our times who gives us a peek at what endures beyond life and death. Emboldening us to live up to our highest potential, he opens the frontiers of human perception, and what could become a doorway to the Divine.

English Publications
Isha Foundation

Sadhguru

LIVING LIFE TO THE FULLEST

"Wherever you are in your life, there is something within you which is longing to be a little more than what you are right now."

Deep within a person is the longing for a human touch, for some sort of connection with another. Thus, a large part of one's life is built on the various relationships that he holds with the people around him.

Here, Sadhguru speaks about the basis of these relationships – how they stem from a common need within every human being. By addressing this need at its very source, he shows the way to know life in its fullest dimension.

For most of you, the way you are right now, the quality of relationships that you hold in your life largely decides the very quality of life that you live. Is that so? So when relationship is playing such an important role in your life, I think it needs to be looked at.

What is the basis of a relationship? First of all, why do human beings need a relationship? Relationships are formed on different levels. There are various types of relationships to fulfill different types of needs. The needs may be physical, psychological, emotional, social, financial, political – they could be of any kind. Whatever the type of relationship, the fundamental aspect of it is that you have a need to fulfill. "No, I have nothing to get... I want to give." Giving is also as much of a need as receiving, isn't it? "I have to give something to someone" – this is also as much a need as "I have to receive something." There is some kind of need. Needs may be diverse, and accordingly relationships could be diverse.

Now for whatever purpose we have formed a relationship, if those needs and those expectations are not fulfilled, the relationship will go bad. We may claim many things, but when your expectations are not fulfilled, it does go bad, isn't it? So instead of being wishy-washy about it, it is best to look at it straight and see what it is, and how we need to handle it.

The needs within a human being have arisen because of a certain sense of incompleteness. People are forming relationships to experience a certain sense of completeness within themselves. When you have a good relationship with someone dear to you, you feel complete. When you do not have that, you feel incomplete. Why is this so? Because this piece of life that you call "myself" is a complete entity by itself. Why is it feeling incomplete? And why is it trying to fulfill itself by making a partnership with another piece of life? The fundamental reason is that we have not explored this piece of life in its full depth and dimension. Although that is the basis of relationships, it is a complex process.

There are expectations, and expectations, and expectations. The expectations that most people are creating are such that there is no human being on the planet who could ever fulfill those expectations. Especially in this man-woman relationship, the expectations are so high that even if you marry a god or a goddess they will fail you. The expectations are so unrealistic that no human being can ever fulfill them. And, without understanding the expectations or the source of the expectations, no one can fulfill expectations. But if you understand what is the source of this expectation, you could form a very beautiful partnership. Are you okay for a joke?

On a certain day, Jack and Jill were going up the hill. Jack had a bucket in his hand, a chicken under his arm, a pitchfork, and a rope at the end of which there was a goat.

Jill said, "I am feeling very nervous."

Jack said, "Why?"

"I am afraid you may have your way with me. I am alone with you."

He said, "What do you mean? I didn't do anything and my hands are full!"

She said, "You could put the pitchfork down, plant it in the earth, tie the goat to it, put the chicken down and put the bucket over it, couldn't you?"

In the process of holding a relationship, at the first moment of meeting, the expectations may be common, but at every step that we take in life, the expectations may become different. These expectations keep changing in people, they are not consistent and they cannot be. One person may be consistent with the same expectation throughout his life; another person's expectations may be changing because his perception and experience of life is changing. Then relationships can become a great conflict.

More conflict is happening within the four walls of the home than anywhere else on the planet. The only thing is bombs are not exploding, so you do not hear it. They may be giving each other silent treatment. It is happening because people's expectations are changing, and they are not changing at the same pace but at different paces.

If you go about doing management and circus with these things, if you constantly try to mind-read the other person and fulfill their expectations, you will become a wreck. There is no way you can gauge it one hundred percent and have a beautiful relationship. You tried those things, isn't it? You have tried to outdo the other person, and in wanting to fulfill all those expectations, you became a wreck. If you go like this, it is an endless circus. To some extent you have to do it, but that is not the basis of a beautiful relationship.

Why have we sought a relationship? If you do not have any kind of relationship in your life, you become depressed. Fundamentally, you are seeking a relationship because you want to be happy, you want to be joyful. Or in other words, you are trying to use the other as a source of your happiness. That means your happiness is not on self-start.

Let us say you bought a car in the 1940s. Along with the car you would have had to get yourself two servants, because morning you need to do push-start. In the 50s if you got a car, one servant would do, because it was crank-start. Now all your automobiles are self-start. But your happiness is still on push-start, isn't it? Someone has to push it a little bit, otherwise it will not get started.

If you put your happiness on self-start, and if you are happy by your own nature, relationships will become a means for you to express your happiness, not to seek happiness. If you are forming relationships to seek happiness – you trying to squeeze happiness out of someone and that person trying to squeeze happiness out of you – this is going to be a painful relationship after some time. But if you have become a joy by yourself, no one is going to complain about you because you are in the process of expressing your joy, not seeking joy from the other person. You can hold a million relationships and still hold them well. This whole circus of trying to fulfill somebody else's expectations would not arise, because if you are an expression of joy, they anyway want to be with you. If you are trying to extract joy from them, then they want to avoid you.

Shifting your life from pursuit of happiness to an expression of joyfulness is what needs to happen if relationships really have to work on all levels – because relationships are of many kinds. Right now, your body is made in such a way that it still needs a relationship. Your mind still needs a relationship. Your emotions still need a relationship. And deeper down, your very energies are made in such a way that you need a relationship on that level also.

If your body goes in search of a relationship, we call this sexuality. If your mind goes in search of relationships, we call this companionship. If your emotion goes in search of relationships, we call this love. If your energies go in search of relationship, we call this yoga. All these efforts are just an attempt to become one with something else. Whether it is sexuality, or companionship, or love, or yoga, you are trying to become one with something else, because somehow, just being who you are right now is not enough.

How can you become one with someone else? Physically you have tried. It looks like you are going to make it, but you know you fall apart. Mentally you have tried many times, you thought you are really there, but you know two minds are never one. No matter what you do with them, no matter how close you think you are, you are never really one. Emotionally you thought you really made it – it gave you the feeling that you really made it, two people have really become one – but lines come up very easily, don't they?

You have tried all these three things. It gives you nearness to that experience, but it does not make you one. There is a longing to become one with something else, because you feel the way you are right now is not sufficient. This longing is not going to stop with just becoming one with one being, because it will long for more and remain a longing forever. The very longing may become a sweet experience for people, and they may get addicted to the longing, but if you really have a longing, then you want to reach the destination someday, you want to reach a fulfillment. And this cannot be fulfilled physically, or mentally or emotionally. So, what is the way to fulfill this longing to become one with something?

Do you know today modern science is telling you that the whole existence is just one energy manifesting itself in a million different ways? When you say $E=mc^2$, you are saying it is all the same energy. "This" and "that" are the same energy; maybe it is not in your perception, but that is the reality, it is a scientific fact. And the religions of the world have been screaming for a long time that God is everywhere. Whether you say God is everywhere, or you say everything is the same energy, it is the same reality expressed in two different ways.

A scientist has not experienced this reality. He has somehow mathematically deduced it. He does not experience this and that as one. A religious person also has not experienced it, but he believes that it is all God.

But a yogi means someone who is not willing to settle for deductions or belief systems – he wants to know it. If you have such a longing that you want to know it, then you have to pursue yoga. The word "yoga" means that in your experience, everything has become one. When I say yoga, don't think I am talking about a particular way of knotting your limbs, or holding your breath, or standing on your head. No. Anything that leads to this union, whichever way, is called yoga. How many ways are there to reach to your ultimate union with life, or with everything? You can only work with what you have.

What is it that you call as "myself" right now? You have a body, you have a mind, you have emotion, and there is an energy which keeps everything going. Your energies may not be in your experience, but you can easily infer and see, if this life has to function like this, there is some kind of energy making this happen, right? We may not understand how this microphone works right now, but because it is amplifying the sound, we can understand that some kind of energy source – either a battery cell, or a power house – is behind this.

These are the four realities for you – body, mind, emotion and energy. All four of them exist every moment of your life. If you employ your body and try to reach your Ultimate nature, we call this karma yoga, the yoga of action. If you employ your intelligence and try to reach your Ultimate nature, we call this gnana yoga, the yoga of intelligence. If you employ your emotion and try to reach your Ultimate nature, we call this bhakti yoga, the yoga of devotion or emotion. If you transform your inner energies and try to reach your Ultimate nature, we call this kriya yoga, the yoga of transforming energies. These are the only four ways you can do it, because these are the only four things that you really have. The rest is imagination; it may be there, but not in your experience.

What is not in your experience is not a reality for you, isn't it? Modern scientists are talking about eleven parallel dimensions happening right here, but that is not in your experience. You can only make a theory out of it, you can only believe it, but it is not yet a reality for you. You cannot work with it. Only when it comes into your experience you can work with it.

So these are the only four realities. If you want to get somewhere, all these four aspects have to function together; only then you get somewhere. With one aspect, you do not get anywhere.

These four dimensions are just head, heart, hands and energy. Is there anyone who is just one big head, no heart at all, no hands at all, no energy? Or one big heart, not the other things? You are a combination of these four things, isn't it? These four things have come together in different ways in every person. Accordingly, the right kind of yoga has to be mixed in the right proportion, otherwise it does not work.

If I give someone one type of yoga it will work miraculously for him, but if I give the same thing to you, it is not going to work because you are not the same combination. This is why the traditions have always insisted on a live Guru, because he mixes the right concoction for you. Unless you mix it properly, the cocktail has no punch.

Because each one is a unique combination of these four things, relationships cannot be managed, but if you handle these four things within you properly, you can include the other as a part of yourself. Instead of trying to manage relationships – which is impossible actually – if you just learn to include the other as a part of yourself, your life becomes an expression of joyfulness not a pursuit of happiness. Then you will see that relationships have various colors, but every color could be enjoyed. Every color and hue that it takes on, could be just fine. In this inclusion, all the differences are okay.

Differences add color and dimension to our lives. The problem with the other person is always that he does not think like you and feel like you. Can you imagine if there was one more person like you in your house, could you live there? That would be a horror! Fortunately, no one else is like you. But that is what you are complaining about – that they are different. You are complaining about what is adding color and dimension to your life because there is no sense of inclusiveness. If you have included the other as a part of yourself, you could enjoy all these differences. Then even if you do not understand what the hell is happening with the other person, still it is okay.

One of our meditators, after a program with us, came back and said, "After all this yoga, now I am able to understand what is my life, but I am unable to understand what is my wife!" You cannot understand, you just have to include. If you make her a part of yourself, you somehow have a wonderful relationship. You do not have to understand every damn thing that the other person is. In fact, they will feel threatened if you understand everything. People are not looking for understanding, though they claim that they are. It is inclusiveness that you are seeking in a relationship.

Wherever there is no inclusion from your side, it is there that people are trouble, please see. Don't try to manage them. Don't try to administer them. People do not like these things. Do you like to be managed by someone? Let's say you thought everything was very spontaneous, and one day you realized somebody has been doing super management on you, would you like it? No. Then why do you think the other person should like it? They also will not like it. Nobody likes to be managed, but everyone longs to be included. Inclusion does not mean you have to go and hug everyone on the street. It is just the way you are, that's all.

If you try to manage relationships with your brilliant management, you will see it will just give you hell. Generally, the smartest people on the planet – those people who think they are really smart – tend to have the most horrible relationships. People who are simple tend to have wonderful relationships, because it is not a question of management. Lots of relationships are going bad, not because of any bad intentions. Most of them go bad with good intentions. Good intentions are unbearable many times!

There was a new lawyer. It was his first case. He was very enthusiastic and he really wanted to do his best. He lost the case. Then he went to meet his client who was in custody.

He told him, "I have good news and bad news for you. Which do you want first?"

The man said, "Okay, give me the bad news first."

The lawyer said, "You have been sentenced to death."

Then the man asked, "What the hell can be good news after this?"

The lawyer said, "I really fought hard and got the voltage reduced for you!"

So good intentions and too much enthusiasm without the necessary sense about the other person can create too many problems in relationships. Managing relationships is not what needs to be done. Relationships are a longing for inclusiveness, and if you approach them as such and include the other as a part of yourself, then however they are, whichever way they are, they will be just fine with you. They will be wonderful for you. Now, relationships will only become a way of looking towards the others' needs, not about your own, because you have no needs of your own anymore. Everyone wants to be with you because your need is gone.

This is the funny thing about life – when you have a need, nobody wants to be with you. When your need is gone, everyone wants to be with you. It is only when the flower blossoms the bees will come. If you do not blossom, bees will not come. If you are a closed bud and call the bees, they will not come. If you open up, you do not have to call, they will anyway come.

If you enhance who you are on all levels – physically, mentally, emotionally, energy-wise – if you enhance yourself into a very beautiful state, everyone wants to hold a relationship with you. Then everything else gets naturally managed. If you do not keep yourself well in any of these levels, and expect people to be with you, then you become a burden.

The problem with us is if we are growing a garden, we are always trying to focus on the flower and the fruit. It is not the flower and the fruit that you should focus on; it is the root. Rather than nurturing the roots, you are constantly seeking the flower and fruit. You do not have to sit here and pray for flowers and fruits. If you nurture the root, the flowers will anyway fall on your head, even if you do not look for them. The flower and fruit will not come if you do not nurture the roots – you can only dream about it. If you nurture the root, flowers and fruits will anyway happen. That is so with the garden, and that is so with your life.

Human beings should always focus on how to enhance their way of being. Whether it is your profession, or your relationship, or whatever else in your life, it will happen to its best only when who you are is enhanced. If you do not enhance this, and you try to manage all those things, it is going to be very stressful. Relationships are probably causing the maximum amount of stress on this planet.

As people get more educated and think they are more modern, they are having more problems having any kind of relationship with anyone. Education should have widened our horizons of life, but it looks like it has compressed everything in such a way that you cannot get along with anyone. This is happening worldwide.

There was a time, and even now in some parts of India, where 200–300 people live together in one large home. Family meant grandfather, grandmother, uncles, aunts, granduncles, grandaunts, cousins – everyone is one family. As we got a little more educated we thought, "These uncles and aunts, damn them." We dropped them. We thought family means husband, wife, children, parents. Then after a while we thought, "My parents are okay, but *her* parents are... let's drown them somewhere." Then we thought, "Let's drop both the parents." We thought family means husband, wife, children. Now the children are thinking differently.

Now it is becoming such that even two people, the couple, are not able to live together. Only if they meet once in a while they are okay. Weekend marriage is all right, but through the week – impossible. It is becoming like that because we are becoming more and more exclusive, not inclusive.

The modern societies are encouraging exclusiveness. Exclusiveness will naturally lead to depression. People are depressed like never before on this planet. Never before has humanity known these kinds of comforts and conveniences. Never before has humanity enjoyed this kind of food security on the planet. Never before has humanity enjoyed this kind of health security. But never before has humanity been this depressed because they cannot get along with anyone. They have become too exclusive.

Inclusiveness is relationship. You know, if I get into a taxi, in a ten-minute ride, by the time I get off, that man will be sharing his whole life with me – because he sees that inclusion in just the way you approach him. You do not treat him as just another person that you use to get somewhere. You treat him as yourself. You treat him as how you would treat the dearest one in your life. Why not? What is your problem? You are seeking a relationship to make your life pleasant; do you want it to be pleasant just those two hours that you spend with someone or do you want it to be pleasant wherever you are? Should your life be pleasant every moment of your life? Then you must spend the time in your life only with people whom you love. Now that is not possible, so the best thing is, just to do that with everyone. There is no scarcity. You know, we have regular programs going on for the last sixteen years in the prisons of South India, and also in a few prisons in the United States. I have a lot of friends who are in! People keep asking me, "Sadhguru, why are you spending so much time with these criminals?" Yes, they have committed all kinds of acts. If you look at their history sheets, there are murders, rapes, drug addictions, and a million other things – every kind of thing that a human being should not do has been done there.

If you let these people out tomorrow morning, maybe at least fifty percent of them will repeat the same things. The other fifty percent of them may look for an alternative way of living, but at least fifty percent will do the same things. This is how they are, but when I am with them, they are absolutely lively, exciting and wonderful people. It is just that if you include someone as a part of yourself, if you are not seeking anything from them and are just a joyful presence for them, people are wonderful. If you meet any kind of person when he is very happy, he is a wonderful person, but if you meet the same person when he is unhappy, he could be really nasty. You are like this too. If someone meets you when you are happy, you are just great. If someone meets you when you are unhappy, it is another game.

Questioner: In my day-to-day life, I just don't get along with people. There seems to be something going wrong with me when I work with people, and I don't know...

Sadhguru: Whatever the nature of your work, probably most of you spend more time at work than with your families, isn't it? Eight to ten hours you are spending with people you work with, but with people whom you are married to, people whom you have borne in your life, you may not be spending that much time. The best part of your day is spent with people whom you work with.

The people whom you work with and what kind of relationships you hold with them is extremely important, because you spend a larger part of your life with them. But most people think in their minds, "This is work, that is life." That means a large part of your life is not life.

Why is this not life? Why are we not looking at this also as an important part of life? Why are we just looking at it as a way to earn something, as a means towards something? The moment you look at work as a means towards something else, slowly your mind concludes that this is not something you are supposed to enjoy as such; this is something that is supposed to be done with. You are looking for when it is time to leave.

Do not divide your life into work and life. It is just life. Every waking moment of your life is just life. Is one moment less important or more important than the other? Is one human being who is sitting next to you less or more important than the other? But you have graded them number one person, number two person, number three person... and that person who is 99 naturally gives you hell!

When whoever is in front of you is not so important for you, in a million ways that person will make your life difficult for no reason, please understand. You do not need to have any particular reason; they will find one. People are quite ingenious about these things. When you are looking at someone, when you are in touch with someone, if within yourself you do not hold this person as truly important for you, you will see that person will come up with a million problems in your life. It is so.

Wherever you are, do not divide your life as work and life.

You have chosen to spend a certain amount of time in different areas according to whatever your needs are. Now once you have decided to be there, it is all life. It is as important as the other, so you throw yourself into it with just as much zest, involvement and inclusion. Then you will not have these problems of "Why is it that people are just getting upset with me?" This problem happens at home, it happens at work, for different people it happens in different places... for some people it happens everywhere.

You need to understand, your ability to hold relationships is not about what types of people are around you. It is about what type of person is here within which gives you the ability to hold relationships. Whether you are with people or without people, it is always best that you spend a little time without people before you impose yourself on them. Put yourself through a little bit of quality control before you impose yourself on other people.

Just spend twenty-four hours by yourself. Don't do anything. Don't read, don't switch on your television, don't sleep. Stay awake, eat well, and sit in one place by yourself. Then you will understand what kind of person this one is. See what all goes through this one's head, through his thought and his emotions. And just see, would you like to hold a relationship with this kind of person? Would you like to meet this kind of person anywhere on the planet?

If not, we need to do something about this one. If you feel this is a wonderful one, this is the kind of person you want to meet, then you go out; anyway you will have wonderful relationships. If you find this is someone that you would like to avoid, then naturally you will be in trouble. Sometimes you may hit it off here and there but never for good.

For short periods of time, any relationship can work, isn't it? Something is being served for both people; so any relationship can work for a short while. When we are talking about managing relationships, we are talking about long-term ways that work. So this is a simple thing you can do with yourself.

Questioner: So, if you spend twenty-four hours with yourself and you do not like what you see, how do you transform that?

Sadhguru: That is good, we have already taken the first step! We need to understand the difference between transformation and change. People are always trying to change themselves. Change means... now this tissue is like this, if I fold it, that is a change. But the essential quality will never change.

When we say "transformation," it means that nothing of the old has remained. Something totally new has flowered within you. Now you look at a rose plant that is full of thorns. Springtime came and rose flowers burst out – it is a transformation. The thorns are still there – there are more thorns than flowers – but we do not call it a thorn plant. We call it a rose plant because of that single rose. Everyone's attention goes more towards that single rose than a hundred thorns that are on the plant, isn't it? So all the thorns in you, maybe you cannot remove them right now, but if one rose flower blossoms, everyone is willing to overlook those things.

You do not have to iron yourself out or straighten yourself out as someone thinks is the right way to be. Those people who have strived to straighten themselves out, they have become so straight that no one wants to be with them. Have you seen this? Someone who is all-correct, do you want to be with that person? Horror, isn't it? This is not about becoming all-correct. No. If you can just make yourself into a very joyful being, whatever other nonsense and quirkiness and kinkiness you have, people are willing to take it.

If you start plucking the thorns, it is an endless process. You need to blossom; at least in one dimension if you blossom, all the other things will be forgotten by people. That is all that needs to happen. So what should we do for that to happen? You cannot pull a flower out of a plant. If you never think about a flower, but every day you nourish the root, then the flower will happen. How to nourish the roots of who you are?

You have a mind, you have emotion, you have a body, but all these things are functioning only because your life energies are functioning. Your heart is beating. Your breath, inhalation and exhalation, is happening. Everything that is life is happening. These life energies are constantly making you tick and happen, and that is what you need to nourish. If you make your life energies properly balanced and in full vibrance, your body, mind and emotion will be in the best possible condition.

There is a whole science and technology as to how to do this. It is this technology that we are referring to as yoga. But unfortunately, the moment I utter the word "yoga," probably people are thinking of impossible physical postures or hanging upside down or whatever. That yoga is a rebound from the American coast. It is "Columbus yoga." You know, even he landed up in the wrong place! But the physicality of yoga is just a small part of it. Yoga is the science and technology of nourishing the roots of your existence so that everything else naturally flowers. Just because you want a flower, a flower will not come. You have to do the right things, only then it happens. That is so with everything in your life. If you do not do the right things, it will not happen.

On a certain winter morning in Michigan, where the lakes freeze such that you can actually drive on the lake, an old timer went ice-fishing. He went at eleven o'clock in the morning, cut a small hole and sat down with a crate of beer next to him – because it is a patience game. He put the line in and sat down, sipping beer, sipping beer, sipping beer. The day went by. By four o'clock in the evening, he still had not caught a single fish. But that is the whole point, to be able to sit there – and old age makes you sit in one place.

Evening, four o'clock, one young boy came, with a big stereo on his shoulders and rap music blaring. He also cut a hole close by and sat down to fish – with the stereo blaring. This man looked at him and thought, "I have been sitting here quietly since morning, and I haven't landed one fish. The fool comes now with a stereo blaring and he hopes to catch fish. Ha! No fool like a young fool." And to his amazement within ten minutes the boy landed a huge trout. He shook his head and looked at it, then he said, "Okay, flash in the pan," dismissed him and again focused on his fishing. Another ten minutes later, the boy landed one more trout. Now he could not ignore him. With great desperation he looked at him. "What is happening? I have been sitting here for the whole day and not caught a single fish. In twenty minutes, the boy has got two!" And to his utter amazement, in another ten minutes, the boy landed one more trout.

Now he could not hold back any more. He kept his pride aside, slowly walked to the young boy and asked, "See, I have been sitting here the whole day not making a single sound, and I haven't landed a single fish. I see in thirty minutes you have three trout in your basket. What is the secret of this?"

The boy said, "Ru Ra Ra Ra Ru Ra Rum."

He said, "What?"

The boy repeated, "Ru Ra Ra, Ra Ru Ra Rum."

The man said, "I don't understand what you are saying."

The boy spat out a blob of something into his hands and said, "You have to keep the worms warm!"

You got to do the right thing otherwise it does not work. If you have stupid morals, principles and ethics, it will not work. Life works only when you do the right thing. With every aspect of life it is true, and so it is true in relationships.

Questioner: Pranam Guruji. After dealing with so many people, I have found that it is not easy to please everyone. So from now on, I live for myself and please myself. Is this a selfish path, or can it be justified in some way?

Sadhguru: Now, you are saying, "Hell with the world, let me please myself." The very fact that you are trying to please yourself means that you are not joyful by your own nature, isn't it? You do not have to please anyone in this world. If you are truly joyful, everyone is pleased by you.

You see a beautiful flower on the plant, it is not interested in pleasing you, but by looking at it you feel very wonderful. When the sun is setting and there is a wonderful color in the sky, do you think the sky is trying to please you? It is just the way it is, and you are pleased by looking at it. If something has become beautiful, it is not trying to make you happy, but you anyway become happy.

You have to make yourself like that. You do not have to please anyone, this is not for someone else's sake. Tell me, how do you want your life to be – pleasant or unpleasant? In body, if you become pleasant, we call this health and pleasure. In mind, if you become pleasant, we call this peace and joyfulness. In emotion, if you become pleasant, we call this love and compassion. In your energies, if you become pleasant, we call this blissfulness and ecstasy. As much pleasantness as possible within you and around you, is this what you want? You become pleasant not for someone else's sake. You want whatever is the maximum level of pleasantness possible in your body, mind, emotions and energy.

If you make yourself utterly pleasant, you will deal with the world to the best of your ability, and that is all we can do. Whether you stand on your feet or on your head, you can deal with it only to the extent that you are capable. But if you are very pleasant, there is very little dealing involved, and you will see relationship is not a problem wherever you go. Because when you are very pleasant, people around you will make everything happen for you. Really! If you are truly pleasant, everyone will take care of you.

See, I travel around the world without a rupee, or a pound, or a dollar in my pocket. Wherever I land, I am well taken care of. Why are these people doing this? I am not going to give them a million because they give me a dollar today. It is just that when you are in the company of utter pleasantness you also become pleasant. And that is what everyone is seeking, isn't it? To be pleasant within themselves, to be pleasant around themselves.

You do not have to please anyone. Don't ever imagine the flowers are trying to please you or anyone. They do not care a hoot for you. But it is their nature to be pleasant, so they are pleasant. Because they are pleasant we want them around. If you are pleasant, everyone would want you around, that is all. You do not have to deal with them, you do not have to be pleasant to people. You do not have to try to be sweet to anyone. If you are just pleasant, whichever way you are, it is fine.

Questioner: *Sadhguru, you were saying that a person should always seek to enhance themselves, and to give joy instead of pursuing happiness. Does this require that we change our thinking on a daily basis? Because I know tomorrow I'll be thinking about the lecture tonight, but when I get up in the morning I don't know how much of the lecture I'll remember.*

Sadhguru: Thought has become very important in today's world. Whatever the nature of your thought, it is functioning only from the data that has already been fed into you. Isn't it so? It is limited data.

Can you make an effort to become more intelligent than the way you are right now? Those people who are trying to be really smart, you always experience them as the most idiotic ones. They are just making fools of themselves most of the time.

You cannot make yourself more intelligent than you are.

Can you make yourself more loving than the way you are?
You may have tried desperately, and people go farther and
farther away from you because you cannot do that either.
Can you make yourself physically more capable than the
way you are? You cannot. Yes, with training you can do
all these things, but I am saying, right now you cannot.

Trying to make yourself more than what you are right
now is not enhancement; it is desperation, and it never
works. When I said enhancement, I did not talk about
this. And now you said tonight you will be thinking about
the lecture. If it runs too strongly in your head you will
not sleep well!

You should not listen to my lecture; you must learn to
listen to the life within you. Life is always longing to be a
little more than what you are right now. Wherever you are
in your life, there is something within you which is
longing to be a little more. So you have to listen to this
one, not to me.

If you listen to me, you will have stories in your head, and
it will not let you sleep tonight. And as you said,
tomorrow morning you will forget it. Or maybe it will run
for three more days and then it will wear out. But the life
within you, non-stop, is constantly striving to be a little
more than what you are right now. If you listen to it, you
will naturally enhance. But your problem is, you are not
life right now, you are just a bundle of thoughts, emotions
and opinions.

Most of the time, you are only thinking about life, not

living life. What can you think about life? Whatever you think about life need not have anything to do with life. Right now, these two hundred people who are sitting here are not in one world; they are in two hundred different worlds. Isn't it so? If they are in two hundred different worlds, does it mean to say that they are in reality or are they are in some kind of a lie? What do you think? You have invented your own, and all your suffering comes from your invention, not from the reality.

What is the kind of suffering that you know? Mental and emotional, maybe sometimes physical. Basically most human beings are going through mental suffering. What happens in your mind, is it your creation? You can say what is happening in this city is not mine, but what is happening in you is definitely yours. If you think "what is happening within me is not mine," then your life is not yours; you better just leave it. If this life is yours, is this mind yours? Now you have a bundle of thoughts in your head, is that yours? Yes. If these thoughts are becoming unpleasant and causing suffering to you, is that yours? Yes, isn't it? So this is just like saying, "If I have money in my pocket, it is mine. If I have credit vouchers, it is not mine." Life does not work like that.

What is happening in your mind is your creation. The world around you is just giving you information. It is throwing pleasant and unpleasant information into you; everything that is happening, it is just throwing it into you. What you do with this damn information is definitely yours.

When the activity of the mind is yours, the suffering that the mind generates is definitely your making. Would you generate unpleasantness and suffering for yourself if your mind was taking instructions from you? No. That means your mind is out of control. If you have an out-of-control mind, do you know what it is called? I do not want to call you names but any instrument in our life is useful to us only if it takes instructions from us.

Right now this microphone, this public address system, is very useful to me because it is amplifying whatever I speak. Suppose it starts saying its own things, I better not be here. And this is what has happened to your mind. It is not doing what you want it to do; it is doing its own things. How can you enhance life when the fundamentals of your life are not taking instructions from you? Let us say you are driving your car, and you want to go here, but it goes there. Is it safe to sit in this car? Is it a useful instrument or is it a nuisance? It is not even a nuisance, it is death.

This mind is not any better. It is worse actually, because you may use your automobile for three or four hours a day, but it is through the vehicle of your mind that you make your whole journey of life. And it is in an out-of-control state. You want to be happy, it makes you stressful. You want to be peaceful, it sets you into a turmoil. Today is your birthday, you want to have the most wonderful time, but it gives you the most horrible time. This is an out-of-control mind. First of all, we have to see how to take charge of this. If you enhance it the way it is right now, it will only enhance the madness.

The very process of your mind is in a compulsive state, not just the expression of it. If we want to go where we want to go in our lives, the first and foremost thing is we must take charge of this body, this mind, this emotion, and this energy. If all these four wheels of your car are in your control, now you can drive this thing wherever you want. If they are not going the way you want to go, if you reach somewhere it must be an accident.

When you exist here as an accident, you are a potential calamity. And because you are a potential calamity, there is anxiety, stress all the time. That is why people have become unhappy. It is not because of relationships that people are unhappy. Take away all relationships and you will see they will become even more unhappy. You cannot be without people, you cannot be with people – this is a problem, a hopeless state. You can be alone and joyful, no problem. Wonderful. Or you can joyfully be with people, wonderful. You cannot be this way, you cannot be that way, then where to send you?

Questioner: What is the purpose of life, Sadhguru?

Sadhguru: You are asking me? The birds are busy gathering their food. Their food is busy trying to escape and live its life. And the cockroaches are busy, or maybe they were busy in the night and now they are resting. Everyone is conducting their life. You are sitting here and thinking, "What is the purpose of life?" Where did you get this problem?

You got this problem because a certain level of intellect was given to you. Now you have this problem of thinking that you are too important on the planet. Human beings are so full of themselves that they think there must be some God-given purpose, a special purpose for them – that too, for each one of them. They are all working at cross purposes and they think they are doing God-given duties.

All those people who believe they are doing God's work, I hope God takes them and gives them some work there, not here. I have been telling him, "Please don't send your soldiers here, keep them there. Why do you send them here? We don't need protection, we are okay as long as it is on. When it is time to die, we will die. If you are so concerned about your security, keep them there." But he keeps sending them here! Conquest, you know, same old problem – imperialism. If God has to send his soldiers to Earth, he is trying to colonize the planet Earth. Not successful, but trying. If you are successful in colonizing a place, you can withdraw the soldiers. If you are not able to withdraw the soldiers it means it has not been successful.

What is the purpose of life? Unfortunately, the so-called religions in the world have filled people with these ideas. One thing I keep hearing everywhere is, "God made us in his own image." Just this idea has rendered humanity into a bunch of vandals. We are walking on this planet like vandals, simply because we think, "We are God's own soldiers here, in his image we have come." If you see, you are just as much as a worm or an insect or a bird or an animal; as they have their life, you have your life. That is a fact, isn't it? You do not know how elaborate a life they have. They have a complete life of their own. Maybe they exist only for two weeks. What you can do in 60–70 years, if someone can do in two weeks, do you call him a genius or not? All this eating, growing up, sleeping, reproducing and dying, they can do it in six days. They are far more efficient than you with life.

This idea that there is something very special about you, and that you must have a special purpose, has destroyed humanity. "Otherwise, how will I do something important?" You do not have to do anything important. These super ambitious idiots who tried to do important things did the most horrible things. If you look at life around you, you just have to do what is needed now. Nothing more.

You think you have a God-given purpose, and now the very life of this planet is threatened in so many ways. There is no creature on this planet which would destroy its own habitat. Even a worm, which probably has a billionth of your brain, is ecologically sensitive. He will never do anything that damages his habitant or his livelihood. But why did our brain, which is so big, get all screwed up? Simply because of these stupid ideas that we have some greater purpose.

Life is the purpose. If this life is not a great enough

purpose for you, please go to heaven soon! If being life, nourishing life, making this life happen in as exuberant a way as you can – if this is not a good enough purpose for you, you must proceed to heaven. So don't look for such purposes. Such purposes have worked at cross purposes with life.

Questioner: Sadhguru, can you define love for us?

Sadhguru: Somewhere, the way the human being is right now, no matter where he is in his life, no matter what he is or what he has achieved, there is a sense of insufficiency. The way he is right now is not enough, he wants to include something else as a part of himself to make himself more complete.

Love is a huge longing to include the other as a part of yourself. That which is not you right now, you want it to become you. It starts from gathering simple things around you, to seeking spirituality or God. The fundamental longing is to have a larger slice of life than what you have right now. You want to experience life little more than the way it is right now. Emotionally, how much ever you make this effort to include the other as a part of you, you get close – you are almost there many moments – but next moment it falls down. It does not matter how intensely you approach it, you will see you are almost there and it falls apart, you are almost there, it falls apart. It gives you a taste of oneness but never establishes you there.

Love is just a vehicle for oneness. What you are longing for is that oneness. Emotion or love is just one more vehicle to get there, but it is a vehicle which takes you close to the other bank and turns you around – it never lands you there. When you get sufficiently mauled by the process of love, you will be ready for Grace.

What do we call as Grace? There are two basic forces within you which are constantly functioning, which seem to be in conflict with most people. They are not in conflict, but most people see them as in conflict. One is the instinct of self-preservation which compels you to build walls around yourself to protect yourself. Another part of you is longing to constantly expand. One is trying to build walls, another is trying to expand.

The walls of self-preservation that you build for today are the walls of self-imprisonment for tomorrow. Many limitations that you establish in your life as a protection for yourself, tomorrow you feel they are imprisoning you, and you want to break them and build a bigger prison for yourself. But day after tomorrow, the same big prison feels like a restriction, and you want to break it and go to the next stage.

These are two longings: one is to preserve yourself, another is to continuously expand. These two things are not opposing forces, but are related to two different aspects of who you are. Self-preservation needs to be limited to the physical body. It is only your body which needs to be preserved, everything else can be mauled and demolished and rebuilt every day. Every day in the morning, you can actually get up and build a whole new personality if you want.

Right now, your instinct of self-preservation has extended itself to the very way you think, feel and understand life. All the time you are trying to protect that, but self-preservation should be limited only to the physical body. Only the body needs preservation, everything else can be reshaped and recreated as you wish any moment of your life. But right now the way you think, the way you feel, your values, your morals, your ideologies, your religion, all these things you want to be preserved. Now in this there can be no expansion. Suddenly, there seems to be a conflict. If only one learns to keep one's instinct of self-preservation just within the ambit of the body and not extend it to other aspects of life, every human being in the planet will naturally be spiritual, will naturally realize his Ultimate nature.

If we have to use an analogy for gravity and Grace, let us put them as opposites. Gravity is one aspect of life which is, in a way, related to the fundamental instinct of self-preservation in a human being. We are sticking to the planet right now because of gravity, otherwise we would be floating all over the place. We have a body today only because of gravity, otherwise we could not have gathered this body itself. So gravity is trying to hold you down, Grace is something that is trying to lift you up. This is only an analogy because Grace cannot be explained that way.

If you are released from the physical forces of existence,

then Grace bursts forth in your life. It is not that Grace has to come – you know always in your calendars and your pictures you saw Grace coming as a few rays of light and reaching a particular person. It is not so. As gravity is active, Grace is constantly active. It is just that you have to make yourself available to it. With gravity you have no choice, anyway you are available to it, but with Grace, you have to make yourself receptive and available to it. So whatever kind of spiritual work you do – whether you do a prayer or *pooja* or *asana, pranayam*, whatever you do – ultimately, you are just working towards making yourself available to the force of Grace, because without Grace you will not be lifted up.

Sadhguru

A FALSE IDENTITY

"The moment you identify yourself with something limited, you are in a natural conflict with the rest of the existence, you cannot help it."

As soon as one is born, a ready-made name is waiting, an identity that follows one throughout their life. Along the way, one picks up many other identities and plays many different roles. Though it creates an individuality, it separates one from the rest of the existence.

In the following exchange, Sadhguru uncovers the roots of these identities and the ensuing conflicts that they create.

Questioner: How to know in any situation what is actually good and what is bad? Because different people have different views about it. How can we live as truly good human beings?

Sadhguru: When you use the word "good," it cannot exist without the opposite of "bad." It is very relative. The moment you say something is good, essentially, you have to make something else bad. The more good I think I am, the more I will think all these other people are not okay. Someone who thinks he is very good, in his mind, nobody in the world will be okay. If nobody in the world is okay, it is not a question of goodness; it is a question of sickness.

It does not matter how much you play it up, how much makeup you apply on the bad and say, "We will accept the bad also" – the idea of goodness has come from considering something else as bad. The more and more you get identified with what you call as goodness, the more and more you will resist what you call as bad. In this resistance, the moment you say, "I am good," you have divided the world into two. The moment you divide the world into two, there is no question of inclusion, there is a certain exclusion.

Now, what is it that we consider as human? If you look at the physical body, we are just animal. This is just biology like any other animal form. So what is it that makes us human? Somewhere within us, there is a certain sense of discretion and discrimination which is not there for the animal. Are you exercising this discretion in every moment of your life or not? This is what makes you a 100% human being or a part-human being, part-animal.

Sometimes the outside situations decide what kind of person you are, isn't it? Right now, if someone in front of you acts nasty, you may act nastier than him. Someone gets angry with you, you get angry with him. Sometimes your chemistry takes over, sometimes your hormones take over, something else takes over, so many forces are ruling you in a compulsive way. These moments you are not really a human being. You are many things in human form.

There are certain moments when you are very conscious, when you are fully aware of what you are doing. Only in those moments do you truly function as a human being. If you were fully aware and conscious of what you are doing with this moment, the way you function in this world and within yourself would be very different. If you were very consciously creating every process of life in you, you would definitely make yourself into a very blissful and ecstatic being. Whenever you are in a state where you are very happy and joyful, you are a wonderful person for everyone around you.

Those moments when you are conscious, definitely you will not create any kind of unpleasantness within you. When you are unpleasant within yourself, you are capable of being unpleasant to someone else. When some unpleasantness is happening within you, knowingly or unknowingly, with good intentions or bad intentions, you will rub this unpleasantness off on other people.

Most unpleasant things on this planet have happened with very good intentions. With the very best of intentions, horrible things have happened. I want you to know even Adolph Hitler had a great intention for the world; he wanted to create a super world. As far as he was concerned, he was just weeding out a few people who were in the way. I want you to understand, in his mind, in his thoughts, and according to his values, he believed that he was creating a super world. So good intentions and you thinking you are good are not sufficient to make life beautiful. You have to become a truly blissful being, only then you will be pleasant to everything around you, not otherwise.

If you are joyful by your own nature – not because of what is happening around you – then if you really want to have a tag of a good human being, you can take it, but I would say it is better you are a joyful human being, not a good human being.

Questioner: In today's world, you see so much terrorism and violence. How do you explain this?

Sadhguru: We need to understand this. Who is a terrorist and who is a patriot? The people whom we worship as patriots, someone else thinks are terrorists. Mangal Pandey is a great patriot for us, we are making movies about him, we celebrate him – but as far as the British were concerned, he was a terrorist, and he was put to death. Bhagat Singh is also a great patriot for us, but he was a terrorist as far as the British government was concerned.

The question is what you are identified with. The moment you identify yourself with something limited, you are in a natural conflict with the rest of the existence, you cannot help it. When it will become violent is just a question of situations.

Right now, if I identify myself with something limited – my community, or my religion, or my nation, or my ideology, whatever – when I will actually become a terrorist and kill somebody is just a question of where I am pushed to in the world. The moment there is a limited identification, there is a conflict. When it actually spills on the street is just a question of time and situations.

It is a limited identification which is making you violent. And every one of you, if you look at your life, you have limited identifications. So whatever you are identified with, whether it is your family or your business or your nation, when it is threatened, you will become violent.

Someone has become a terrorist and is willing to blow himself up simply because his identification is limited, either with a nation, or a religion, or a particular sect, or whatever. If only this limited identity was not there, if he identified himself as just a human being, or as just a life form, then with whom would he be violent? Naturally, this passion would find beautiful expressions.

The passion itself we do not want to kill; it is wonderful because that is what makes a human being worthwhile. Otherwise we will be just worthwhile wimps, no good for anything. I want you to understand, people who are exploding bombs are not evil people. All these terrorists, people who are willing to die for what they believe in, are wonderful people, it is just that they have been misguided to do things in a certain way. It is really wonderful, but how unfortunate that such wonderful people are being used like this in a life-negative way. If only this passion found a gentler expression, this would be a fantastic quality among people. What we need to look at is just the expression, the way they are expressing their passion.

Questioner: Is this limited identity coming from one's culture?

Sadhguru: Culture is something that we need to enjoy. We should not destroy the culture in which we live. Whatever the culture is, each one of us should keep the culture – that makes life colorful and worthwhile to go around. Otherwise, if all of us were the same uniformed people, life would not be interesting around us. But the limited identity is not coming because you are identified either as a Hindu or a Muslim or Indian or Pakistani or this or that; it is starting with your physical body.

When you were born your body was so small, now it has become so big. That means you accumulated it slowly. What you call as your physical body is an accumulation. It is a piece of planet that you picked up and made into this. Similarly, what you call as my mind is a huge accumulation of impressions of life around you. Depending upon what kind of social, educational, religious and family situations, accordingly, you have taken in those kinds of impressions, and you formed a certain kind of mind.

Both your physical body and your mind are accumulations. What you accumulate is definitely not you, isn't it? It is yours, I am not disputing that, but it is not you. So the moment you start identifying yourself with the accumulations that you call as body and mind, and with the process of accumulating, all other identifications follow the same way, you cannot help it.

If you want to become free from other limited identifications that you have... you may try to shake off your Indian-ness, or your Hindu-ness, or your Muslim-ness, or whatever else, it does not go no matter what you do. If you drop that, you will identify with something else. Suppose you drop your religion, you will identify with your class, or with your community in some way – because the basic identity, the wrong identification has started with the physical body and mind.

What we refer to as a spiritual process is just that in your experience you create a distance between you and your physical body, between you and your mind. You learn to 'use these two accumulations well, but you do not get identified with them. The moment you are not identified with these two, you will not be identified with anything. You can play your game whichever way you want in the world, but you will not get entangled.

You know, always the so-called spirituality has been talking about detachment. Why? Because you are afraid of involvement. You think that if you are involved, you could get hurt. If you are involved, you will not get hurt; if you are entangled, you get hurt. It is the entanglement which causes the pain and suffering, not involvement.

People have generally known only entanglement, not involvement. Without involvement there is no life, isn't it? Can you experience anything without involvement? Whether it is the food that you eat, or the people around you, or the life around you, or art, or music, or whatever in your life – you cannot experience it without involvement.

Where there is no involvement, there is no possibility of any depth of experience in your life. But people have been always telling you about detachment because they are afraid of entanglement. They think if they get involved, they will get entangled. Because people cannot distinguish between involvement and entanglement, a simple blatant solution seems to be detachment. But detachment is not a solution for life. It is a way of avoiding life. If you want to keep away from life, you just have to fall dead, it is very simple. If you want to stay away from life, why are you trying to be alive and stay away from life? Just fall dead, your objective is fulfilled.

The fundamental basis of entanglement is that you are identified with things that you are not. The moment you are identified with something that you are not, entanglement is inevitable. Wherever you put your hand, it will stick to you. There is no other way. When you sit here now, in your experience if it is clear-cut within you that your body sits here, your mind is out there, and what is you is away from both – if a distinct separation is there from this, would you get entangled with anything in your life?

Only because you are attached to this body, only because you are entangled with this body, you get entangled with "every-body." If you are not attached and entangled with this body, you will not be entangled with "any-body." You can throw yourself into anyone's life with total involvement without the fear of entanglement. Now you are afraid to talk to this person and get involved – "Suppose this person does something else tomorrow, will I be hurt?" If there is a possibility of entanglement and pain attached to it, definitely you would hesitate to get involved. When there is no fear of entanglement, that is when you would throw yourself into everything.

Questioner: *Then shouldn't we make efforts to bring some values into people? That way, we could avoid this violence and conflict in the world.*

Sadhguru: Why are we sticking to some values? This is fundamentally because there is no consciousness, there is no inner experience, yes? If your humanity is in full flow this moment, why would you need values? Why should I tell you, "Be good to this person." If your humanity is fully active this moment, do I have to teach you, "Please be nice to this man, don't kill him"? Only because you are identified with something and are suppressing the basic humanity in you, now we have to tell you, "Please don't kill this man, be good to this man. Okay, he is some other caste, some other creed, but please be good to him." This kind of teaching is necessary simply because we have suppressed the basic nature within us. If your humanity is in full flow, at that moment, nobody has to tell you what is right and what is wrong. Whichever way you are, you will be fine.

Whether it is old values, new values, or whatever, at no time in the history of humanity have all the people had the same values. Always, one person's values and the values of the person sitting next to them are different. Even within a family of two people, two people do not share exactly one hundred percent the same values. If I stand by my values and you stand by your values, conflict is inevitable. This is the basis of conflict.

All values and moralities have come into the social sphere only because the inner dimensions have not found full flowering. When the interiority of a human being does not find full expression, when it is somehow suppressed by various means, that is when we have to teach people what is right, what is wrong, what is okay, what is not okay.

The whole spiritual process or yoga is just about this. The word "yoga" means union. Union between what and what? There is something called as "me," there is something called as the "other," which is the basis of all conflict in the existence. This "me" and "the other" can get extended to groups of people, communities, nations and various types, but fundamentally, "me" and "the other" is the basis of conflict in the universe.

What is "me," and what is not "me?" Right now, what are the things which you call as "myself?" Your thoughts, your emotions, your body, your ideas, your philosophies, this is what you call as "me," isn't it? All these things you accumulated from outside, they are not you. If your experience of life transcended the limited accumulations that you have made in your life in the form of body, in the form of thought, in the form of emotion, and ideologies, and philosophies, and values, then there is no such thing as "me" and "you," and there would be no conflict.

The whole aspect of yoga, or spiritual process, is to bring you to this experience that if you sit here, there is no such thing as "you" and "me." It is all me, or all you. For one moment, right now, if you experience all these people who are sitting here really as a part of yourself, after that do I have to teach you morals and values – "Be good to this person, don't harm this person, don't kill this person?" It would not be necessary for you. Only because you have created a false sense of identity about yourself, we have to teach values and values.

If you want to go beyond this, if you want to live here without values, then your consciousness has to flower, your humanity has to find full expression. Even for a single moment in your life, if you start experiencing these people as how you experience the ten fingers of your hand, after that I do not have to teach you any values or morality about anyone. With that which you have known as yourself, you have no conflict. The conflict is always with the other.

Questioner: So many things do not seem to be in our control. Are they happening because of our karmic background or according to a Divine plan?

Sadhguru: For every simple physical reality that we face, we are always looking for a mystical solution. This is endemic in India, you know. Because the land has seen so much of mysticism, the common people in the country have started giving mystical reasons for every little thing that happens. You do not pass an examination – gods are working against you. Rains do not come, gods are angry with you. A big wave comes, something else is happening in heaven. These are simple physical realities which need to be handled physically.

Now what is karmic, what is not karmic? Your very existence here is karmic. The word "karma" literally means action. We are talking about your action. When it comes to action, you can perform action in four different ways. You can do physical action, mental action, emotional action and energy action. In all these four levels, action is constantly happening. Some of it you are consciously doing, but a large part of it is unconsciously happening. The imprint of this action that you perform in these four dimensions is always left within you as a residue. These imprints gather over a period of time and they develop their own tendencies.

Let us look at it this way. From the moment you were born to this moment, every kind of action that you have performed in your life – physical, mental, and emotional – is it not deciding what happens to you and how you are right now? Whichever way your karma is, that is the kind of person you are right now. From the moment you were born, what kind of family, what kind of parents, what kind of school, what kind of friends, where you went, where you did not go, what you did, what you did not do until this moment – is it not deciding the very way you think, feel, understand and experience your life right now? This is karma.

Karma is a software that you wrote for yourself unconsciously. Depending upon the type of actions that you perform in your mind, in your emotion, in your body and in your energy, accordingly you write your software. Whichever kind of software you wrote, after some time that is how this whole mechanism functions. Once you write a certain type of software, now this whole system functions only that way. It is not written by some other dimension or force; it is written by you, but because you did most of it unconsciously, you cannot believe you did it.

You went up a mountain, and as you were walking down, you only dislodged one small pebble. This pebble rolled down and slowly became a huge avalanche and wiped out a whole village. Now you cannot believe you did it, because you just dislodged a single pebble, but it has picked up momentum.

If you can write a software unconsciously, you can also write it consciously. Spiritual process is about re-writing your software consciously. Somehow you wrote it unconsciously. Now that you have become aware enough, why not write it consciously?

If you wrote it consciously, you would not write a software of disaster, a software of pain, a software of suffering, anger and hatred. Definitely you would write a pleasant software for yourself, not an unpleasant one. Nobody is seeking to be unpleasant consciously, but people are becoming unpleasant in so many ways because a large part of them is still unconscious, compulsive.

You are happening as a compulsive being, not as a conscious being. That is the basis of all unpleasantness in a human being. If you had written your software consciously in your life, definitely you would have written a software of ecstasy and blissfulness, not a software of pain, suffering, tension and frustration in your life. This is karma.

Karma is not deciding about what happens. Karma is deciding how you experience your life. The quality of your life is always decided by how you experience, not by what you have around you. You can sit in a palace and be utterly miserable. You can be on the street and be joyful. It is the quality of your experience, not what you have, which decides the quality of your life. What you have just brings convenience to you, that's all.

Questioner: *So is this something like destiny?*

Sadhguru: A hundred years ago, whatever things people thought of as destiny, today many of those things you have taken into your hands isn't it? Whatever your grandmother thought was destiny, you have taken it into your hands and are making it happen the way you want.

All the things that we do not understand, all the things that we are not able to logically compute, we are always calling destiny. It is convenient. All the things which are unpleasant in us, we are blaming it on destiny – "We are like this because our destiny is like this." We do not want to admit that we are like this because *we* are like this. Your destiny is written by you unconsciously.

How much out of control you are, that is how much destiny you will talk about. If you have mastery over your physical body, 15-20% of your life and destiny will be in your hands. If you have mastery over your mind, 50-60% of your life and destiny will be in your hands. If you have mastery over your life energies, 100% of your life and destiny will be in your hands.

Questioner: *So is there such a thing called the Divine plan? Do we have a choice? What's the role of free will in this?*

Sadhguru: About the Divine plan, I must tell you something. I happened to be in an international conference where people were discussing about poverty alleviation, about hunger in the world, about how we can influence the world leaders and the governments to do something about people who are dying without the basic thing called food. One person stood up – supposedly a very responsible person in the world – and said, "Isn't this all Divine plan, that 50% of the people should eat well and 50% of the people should starve to death? Is this not all Divine plan?"

Now I could not just sit there. If someone else is hungry, someone else's children are dying without food, it must be Divine plan, but if your stomach is empty, you will definitely have your own plan as to how to fill it up! Is this not so?

Somehow in the name of divinity we have just lost our humanity. Don't talk about divinity, let your humanity overflow. When your humanity overflows, you will touch divinity, otherwise there is no way. It is simply empty talk; it doesn't get anyone anywhere.

Too much God in this world, that has been the biggest problem, isn't it? Everyone is talking about God simply because they have not realized the immensity of being a human being. The immense potential of being a human being has not been understood or experienced, that is why for anything that is a little good they say "it is Divine."

Human is a tremendous possibility; it can touch the very peak. Do you know in our culture they say if God had problems he came down to visit the sages for consultation? Do you know many stories like that? That shows that human is a much bigger possibility. Because people have not realized the immensity of their humanity they are all the time talking about divinity. I want you to overflow with your humanity first, then we will see about divinity.

Questioner: But what about surrender then? There is so much talk about surrender in this journey. Doesn't it mean we should surrender to the Divine plan?

Sadhguru: Surrender is not to anything. Surrender is a simple art of keeping yourself aside. You are too full of yourself, if you know how to keep yourself aside in the way you exist, or at least in the way you act, this is what you are referring to as surrender. Someone has surrendered to power, someone has surrendered to work, someone else has surrendered to something else. You learn to keep yourself aside. If you know how to keep yourself aside completely, then suddenly a totally different dimension starts functioning within you.

Questioner: So we're talking about that non-identification?

Sadhguru: Yes. The ultimate surrender is that you are not identified with your own body and with your mind, with your ideas, with your emotions. Once you keep this aside, a completely new dimension begins to function within you. If you want to call it Divine, you call it Divine. If you want to call it God, you call it God. If you want to call it Shiva, you call it Shiva. You can call it whatever you want, but that which is the basis of creation becomes active within you.

Right now when you are identified with the body and mind, you are just a piece of creation. The moment your identity is taken off from this, suddenly an explosion of what you call as the Creator begins to happen to you. Now, the fundamental question is "How can this happen within me unless I look up at heaven and invite God to make it happen to me?"

When you were born you were so small, now you have become this big. You did not go for weekly stretching, did you? The body is being created from inside. You are providing it the food, but where is it being created from? Definitely from within. The manufacturer of this body is within, that means the Creator is within, constantly functioning. It is just that you have ignored him for too long because you are too identified with the physical and the mental aspects of yourself.

The whole idea of God and Divine has entered your mind only because you have seen the creation. You came out of your mother's womb and looked around, there was so much creation already. Obviously, you did not create it. Who created it? You looked at your mother, your father, this man, that man – nobody had the face who could fit into that dimension that they could have created all the magnificent creation around you. Then you naturally looked up.

Your idea of God has come to you only because some experience of the creation came to you. It is because you saw the creation that you thought up a Creator. So what is the Creator? What kind of Creator do we have, is it a man or a woman, or is it an animal, is it half an animal, half man? What is it? Every culture has its own idea of what the Creator looks like.

If you want to experientially approach this, the only doorway to the Creator is the creation, and the closest piece of creation to you is yourself. With everything else there is a certain distance.

If you want to approach the Creator, definitely turning inward is the best way, but what means do you have to turn inward? All you have are sense organs, which are essentially outward-bound. You can see what is outside, but you cannot roll your eyeballs inside and see what is within. If an ant crawls up on your skin, you know it. But so much blood is flowing, do you experience it? This dimension has not come into your experience because sense organs are essentially outward-bound.

If you want to go beyond the limitations of five sense perceptions, the physical body should evolve to its next stage. The mind should evolve, and the emotion and the energy should move. These are the four realities in your life, what you consider as "myself." These are the four wheels which you have to learn to move. You can use these four dimensions to go ahead.

You have to transcend the limitations of the senses, only then the inner dimension becomes a reality; otherwise it is just a fairytale. Once a fairytale is told, it can get exaggerated from generation to generation to such ridiculous heights – which has already happened in so many ways. Whether you seek it here or there or in whatever form, ultimately what you are seeking is that which is the source of creation. When you say Divine or God, you are talking about a dimension which is the basis of all creation. If you are seeking this, the best place to seek it is definitely within you, not somewhere else.

Questioner: Can reading scriptures, like the Bhagavad Gita for instance, help one experience this divinity?

Sadhguru: I am not saying this with any disrespect or demeaning it, but all scriptures in the world – it does not matter how they came – were written by a human being, isn't it? It does not matter if God himself spoke, it was still written by a human being.

Questioner: But still what was written in the Gita, what Krishna spoke thousands of years ago, is still relevant for millions of people today. He set an example for us to follow. Can't we have trust in him?

Sadhguru: How do you know that Krishna is not the biggest liar in the world? When you have problems trusting the man who is sitting next to you, how can you trust a man who was 3,500 years ago? Just because everybody is shouting slogans, "Jai Krishna, Jai Krishna" it does not mean anything.

And can you call Krishna a good man? He definitely does not fit into any ideas, any values or any morality that you have in your life. If you go by what Krishna says by the word, it will end you up somewhere else. Right now, we are talking about Krishna because there is a distance of time. Suppose there was a man like Krishna in your neighborhood – you would have huge problems even accepting him, forget about worshiping him.

Questioner: Why?

Sadhguru: Why, because if you sleep off in the middle of the night, your wife will go and dance with him! Your daughter will go and dance with him. Your eighty-year-old mother also wants to go dance with him.

Let us understand this, whatever happened between Krishna and the gopis is not seen by the society as something Divine. Whatever happened in a certain consciousness between two people is not understood and experienced by the other people.

Even then, Radhe's sister again and again plotted to kill Krishna, you know that? Today, their love affair is hugely celebrated: she is a married woman and she is having a roaring affair with this man. Definitely the society wants to kill him. It was so then, and even now it is so. Maybe it is taking them to a different dimension – that is between the two of them – but as far as the social scene is concerned, it is a huge scandal. Even then it was a scandal, even now it is a scandal. Between the two of them, something beautiful is happening, that is different.

If Krishna comes alive in your neighborhood… if your neighbor's child comes and raids your refrigerator, will you think he is enlightened? This is what Krishna did! Today all of it is romance, all of it is wonderful, but in reality, in your life if it happens, things would be very different.

When you say scriptures, it does not matter what Krishna said, it is someone else who wrote it down. Human minds are given to enormous distortion. This is a reality. Right now we are sitting here and I am speaking; in half an hour's time when you leave this hall, each one of you will have a different version of what I have spoken. I am one hundred percent certain about that. Whatever the human mind produces, there is bound to be distortion.

I am not saying these scriptures are worthless or useless. Maybe they are of enormous value, you don't know, but they were written by human beings. But *this* book, what you call as "me" was written by the Creator himself. When *this* book is alive and kicking, written by the Creator himself where there cannot be a mistake – does you reading some other book to know yourself make sense?

If you are serious about making any journey, you must be willing to start from the seat where you are sitting. If you try to start from the other end of the town, your whole life will go in hallucination. You can only start from where you are sitting right now. If we really want to take a step in our lives, the first thing is to identify where we are, and what is the next step. You cannot start from the Supreme being. You have to start from you.

So leave the things that you believe, leave the things that you have read, leave the things that you have heard. What is it that you know experientially about life and yourself? And what is it that you do not know? You will see you may know many things about the physical realities in the world. You may know many things about this city and how to manage your life here, but you will see, you do not know anything about yourself.

Right now if you do not know, it is most important that you see that you do not know. "I do not know" is a tremendous possibility. "I do not know" is the basis of all knowing in the existence. If you destroy "I do not know" with conclusions and beliefs and whatever else, you destroy all possibility of knowing. If you believe it, you will not get anywhere, if you disbelieve it, you will not get anywhere. All you will have is a conclusion to talk about. It will solace you for today, but it will not lead you to liberation. It will not lead you forward one inch, existentially.

If you are just looking for a little bit of solace and comfort, all these things will work. But if you are looking for the Ultimate nature of who you are, then all these things will not help. The only way is to turn inward. You can read about Krishna, or a Jesus, or Buddha and how wonderfully they lived just as an inspiration. You do not know for certain, but they seem to be living beyond the limitations in which you exist.

All books, all philosophies, all people that we talk about are only inspirations to go beyond our limitations. Once you are sufficiently inspired, books are of no consequence. You have to turn inward because here is a book written by the Creator himself. Ignoring that, you are reading a book that is written by a human being. You have to turn inward.

Questioner: Being a Hindu, I'm often asked "What is Hinduism?" and I find myself lost. So many gods and goddesses, such vastness – can you please give a definition of Hinduism?

Sadhguru: The word "Hindu" comes from the word "Sindhu." Sindhu is a river. The civilization that was born on the banks of this river was called the Sindhu civilization. When the Persians came they could not pronounce "Sindhu," so they called it "Indu." Over a period of time, it became "Hindu."

Hindu is a geographical identity and to some extent a cultural identity. It is not a religious identity; Hindu was never an "ism." It is only when hugely aggressive, competitive religions came, the Hindus tried to organize themselves as a religion, but even now they are not successful – because there is no one belief system. There is no belief system at all.

You can believe that God is a man and be a good Hindu. You can believe God is a woman and be a good Hindu. You can believe God is a monkey and be a good Hindu. You can believe God is a cow and be a good Hindu. You can worship a snake and be a good Hindu. You can worship a tree and be a good Hindu. And if you do not worship anything, you can still be a good Hindu, because it is a geographical and cultural identity. It is not based on any particular belief system.

This culture, over a period of time, focused its whole attention on the ultimate development and wellbeing of the human being. The immediate wellbeing was not too important; the ultimate wellbeing became the most important for them.

These days you have forgotten this, but generally it is said that for a Hindu there is only one goal in life: *mukti*. Mukti means liberation. For a Hindu, his business, his career, and his family are all secondary things – they are only stepping stones towards his Ultimate liberation. Even God is just one more device for him to attain to his Ultimate liberation. No one else looks at it this way.

Generally in every religion, God is the ultimate goal. But this is a culture where we do not see God as the ultimate thing because we understand that we created him. And we can create any number and kind of gods that we want. We learned this whole art and science of consecration, with which we can make a rock into the Divine.

Let us say you ate chicken in the afternoon. In one afternoon, the chicken is becoming a human being, isn't it? According to Darwin's theory of evolution, from a chicken to a human being, so many million years passed. But in a single afternoon you are transforming a chicken into a human being in your body. This process is called digestion.

If you go further backwards, if you take manure and put it at the root of the plant, maybe in a month's time it becomes a sweet apple. It is just a lump of shit that is hanging there. So sweet and wonderful, but it is the same thing. This is called cultivation or agriculture, where you are converting one thing into another.

Similarly, you can convert a stone into Divine; this is called consecration. This science was explored in a huge way, and people learned how to create very intense forms of energy, which are way beyond where a human being is right now.

Today science is proving to you that everything is the same energy. The difference between a rock and you is a different level of intensity and function, isn't it? And religions have always been saying that God is everywhere. If God is everywhere, a chair is also God, and this body is also God. But it is not the same thing in its function. What is in its ultimate function and ultimate possibility, you call as God. What is in its lowest function, maybe you will call it a rock or something else. But it is the same energy. To transform something into that ultimate possibility, is what the science of consecration is about.

This science was explored and they started manifesting the Divine in a million different ways, whichever way they liked. If you look at in how many ways it has been done, it is absolutely incredible. Even people who are living in India have unfortunately not explored it, and it has been hugely lost these days. But if you explore the deeper dimensions of this culture in terms of what has been done for inner wellbeing, nowhere else has humanity invested that much time and energy to look at the inner wellbeing of a human being.

I think one person who put this forth very beautifully was Mark Twain. Mark Twain had heard so much about Indian mysticism that he traveled to India and spent a little over three months there. He had a good guide who took him to the right places. And before he left or just after he went back, he said, "So far as I am able to judge, nothing has been left undone, either by man or nature, to make India the most extraordinary country that the sun visits on his rounds. Nothing seems to have been forgotten, nothing overlooked." And much more has been done. If you explore the mysticism in India, it is so incredible that you will not believe that it has happened on this planet. Because this does not come from a belief system. It happens as a science. Because of this, you cannot call Hindu as a religion. It is a way of life, it is a culture, it is a geographical identity which is desperately trying to organize itself as a religion because of extra competition that has come. But they will never manage because there is no one particular belief system to organize people around it.

In other words, what Hindu way of life means is everyone can have their own religion. That is, in your family, if there are five people, five of you can have your own religion. You can worship the monkey, another person can worship the snake, another person can worship the cow, another person can worship the tree, whatever he likes. Whatever he can relate to, he can worship that; or if he has no need for worship, he need not worship and he is still a good Hindu. I think this is the freedom and sense that we need in the world today. The conflict in the world has always been projected as good versus bad, but it is not so. The conflict has always been one man's belief versus another man's belief.

First of all, why do you believe something? Because somewhere you have lost the fundamental sincerity to simply accept what you do not know as you do not know. Everything that you do not know, you have to believe. If you see "I do not know," you cannot fight with anyone. You believe "This is it," that is when you fight with somebody. Belief gives you a certain sense of confidence and stability, but it is a dangerous confidence. Confidence without clarity is a deadly mix.

I do not want to make political statements, but you manufacture these presidents of powerful countries when you have too much confidence and no clarity. And this comes from belief. When you believe something that you do not know, it gives you enormous confidence. It looks like power, it looks like strength, but it is always a destructive strength. You do not need any confidence in your life. What you need is clarity. How much clarity you have with life, only to that extent you can handle it.

Sadhguru

ORDINARY TO EXTRAORDINARY

"To have the awareness that we are only moving from one form of ignorance to another, is the greatest blessing that one can start with right now."

In a world where "knowledge is power," ignorance is considered the depth of inferiority. Right from childhood, we are trained to believe that the more we know, the better a human being we become. In the following chapter, Sadhguru leads us to the freedom of being "absolutely ignorant" – unfathomable for today's culture and mindset.

What is real and what is not? Assumptions and preconceived conclusions crumble, and the line becomes hazy between illusion and clarity, between ignorance and enlightenment, and between the ordinary and extraordinary, as Sadhguru takes the seeker from the limited scope of words and ideas, to the unlimited possibility beyond any language.

The furthest limits of ignorance is not reached because of effortful thought, nor is it reached because of good deeds that one can perform, but only because of the mindless ecstasy that is set forth because of a vibrant one. This mindless ecstasy takes you to the very boundaries of your ignorance, at the same time it also reveals the bond that keeps you as a limited self. Everything is just ignorance. What we call as knowledge is just ignorance. One can just move from one level of ignorance to another until he becomes willing enough to fall into the Ultimate oblivion of a Realized one.

Ignorance means different things to different people. If you have not heard of him before, Tenali Ramakrishna was a very humorous bard in the court of a South Indian king who built a huge empire in this part of the world. Because he came from the village named Tenali and his name was Ramakrishna, generally he was known as Tenali Rama.

On a certain day, he was sitting with a group of people and discussing some philosophical matters. But there was one man, who was just outside the circle, who went on making irrelevant comments. After some time Tenali Rama couldn't take it anymore.

He said, "You are a fool! You are a good-for-nothing, and you are nothing!"

That man was stung by the insult. He said, "How can you say I am nothing?"

Tenali Rama repeated, "Yes, you are nothing. You are really nothing."

"How dare you say I am nothing! I am the town's cobbler."

Tenali Ramakrishna picked up his footwear, tore it, and threw it at him and said, "If you are really the cobbler, fix this and make it like new." That man immediately picked up the footwear and left to fix it.

When someone says you are nothing, if you are a cobbler, it is an insult. If you are truly into meditation, that would be the truth for you. Ignorance is always in many different layers and boundaries.

Life continues to be a mystery; it has always been, still is, and it always will be. At different times we have thought different things are mysterious. The borders of our ignorance may be enhanced over a period of time. In these millions of years of human evolution on this planet, definitely our brains have grown, become more capable of intellectual processing and perception. With all this evolution, life has become only more mysterious, not less.

Maybe a thousand years ago, we did not know how this body functions. Now, we have opened it, looked at it, done so many things with it; we know many things. The more and more we get to know about this, it is only becoming more and more mysterious, like never before. A thousand years ago, if you looked up in the sky with your naked eye – I don't know if anyone has counted, but maybe there are five to ten thousand stars up there that you could see and count. Today, we have powerful telescopes with which we have looked beyond this, now we know there are billions of stars. It is only getting more mysterious and more complicated.

Science is supposed to bring clarity to your life. But today modern physics is creating more confusion, and it sounds more mysterious than mysticism. The mumbo-jumbo of mysticism sounds reasonable compared to what modern physics is talking about today. An Einstein sounds much more unreasonable than a Harry Potter! Because they are talking in totally mysterious ways. And as our perception and so-called knowledge increases, life is becoming only more and more mysterious.

All that we are doing is pushing the borders of our ignorance, making it larger and larger. Today modern science is saying this is an ever-expanding universe. If you have to expand, you need some space to expand into. If it is ever-expanding, what is it going to expand into? It is a continuous mystery. Unless you become an absolute void by yourself, you will not know the depth of your ignorance.

Enlightenment is not a knowing; enlightenment is touching a borderless ignorance. Everyone's ignorance has a border. An enlightened being's ignorance is borderless, boundless. When life happens in limited ways, everything seems to be clear. When things beyond your limitations begin to happen, nothing is clear anymore.

Those of you who have been on the path... The word "path" is a deception, because a path is supposed to take you somewhere. But you are only getting more and more lost. Maybe a little joyfully lost, but lost. If you get completely lost, when you see there is no hope of getting anywhere, that is it. It is only because you are trying to get somewhere you can be lost. When you realize that you are absolutely, hopelessly lost, then you are just fine. If your ignorance crosses all boundaries, when you become utterly ignorant, you are fine. Utterly ignorant means you have become empty. Emptiness is ignorance. The ultimate ignorance is Shiva: "that which is not." "That which is" is some kind of knowing.

As long as one is in pursuit of something or the other, it is an endless process. As long as we are getting identified and attached to different situations we get into – however beautiful the situation may be – the moment you think "this is it," you are trying to freeze yourself into a certain state of ignorance. When you realize that every peak is only a launch pad for the next peak, and that the next peak is not the goal or the destination, then the only thing that can be the destination is an Ultimate oblivion. That sounds very negative and uninspiring for anyone – not a destination that anyone would want to seek. People would like to go to heaven, people would like to sit in sweet places, sit in God's lap, do pleasant things. To have the awareness to know that we are only moving from one form of ignorance to another, is the greatest blessing that one can start with right now.

Once there was a yogi who sat in a temple yard. There were moments when he was godlike; then people gathered and started worshipping him. Next moment he would be like a madman; then people went away thinking they made a mistake. Like this, he was alternating between one thing and another all the time.

One particular householder, who was a regular to the temple, got drawn to this yogi. He saw that the yogi did not eat for many days if no one served him. So he took it upon himself; every day he cooked food and brought it for the yogi. Until he ate, he just sat there, he himself not eating. Then he ate what was left over. He made this his life, and he made this his mission. The yogi sometimes ate in the morning, sometimes ate in the afternoon, sometimes the evening, sometimes the next morning. You never know when he eats, but this man dedicated himself to this one task: cooking food, bringing it for him, until he eats he does not eat. He waited and waited.

This went on for some time, a few years. One day, the yogi took a certain fondness to this man and he said, "From tomorrow I will come to your house. You don't bother to come. You cook the food and be ready, I will come to your home and eat it there."

The man said, "Okay."

He went home and the next day he prepared food and waited. He was sitting and waiting, but the yogi did not turn up. Then a dog was bothering him; it was trying to smell and go near the food. He chased it away many times, but it kept coming back. So he took a stick and gave a nice beating to the dog. The dog moved away, stood back, tears appeared in its eyes, and it went away. Then until evening he waited, the yogi did not come.

He went to the temple, and the yogi was just sitting there,

tears flowing from his eyes. The man was disturbed. He said, "You said you would come home, and I waited and waited. And why the tears? You said you would come, that's why I waited. Otherwise I would have come."

The yogi said, "I came many times to your house – twelve times, to be exact, I tried to enter your house. You abused me, you chased me, then you beat me up, so here I am." Then the man realized the dog actually tried to enter the house twelve times.

A master need not always come in the form of a small white swan, as it has been written in the legends; he may come as a dog. If you get too attached to a particular form, experience or state within yourself, you will miss the whole point. To progress in one's path simply means that you have an expanded sense of ignorance.

All these years, scientists believed that someday we would know what is the nature of existence. But today, a lot of top-level physicists are beginning to talk in terms of how we will never know; we will just go on expanding the borders of our ignorance, but we will never know. This is what mysticism meant. A mystic means an utterly ignorant person. Everyone else is a little bit ignorant, a little bit knowledgeable. They know some things, they do not know some things. Someone who does not know anything at all, who is not burdened by knowledge, is a mystic. Knowledge is an accumulation. Someone who is simply not burdened by any kind of accumulation is a mystic, because he has chosen to be utterly, absolutely ignorant, not in parts.

Once it happened, a man was trying to carry a huge grandfather clock from a truck to his house, on his back.

A drunk came by and said, "Hey mister, you just take my advice: get yourself a wristwatch."

If you are carrying a grandfather clock on your back, it may have great value, but you cannot even look at the time. You have to ask someone, "Please look at the time and tell me, what's the time?" Aren't you slowly becoming like this these days? "How am I?" Sensible people ask, "How are you?" Now, a lot of people are coming up to me and asking me, "Sadhguru, how am I?" I'm supposed to enlighten! What to do?

Questioner: Namaskaram Sadhguru. This is the first time that I am staying for a week in the ashram.[1] Sometimes I feel comfortable and want to stay here, but at other times I feel uncomfortable and want to go home. I am so confused. Please guide me about what I want to do.

Sadhguru: Generally, everyone feels this way. When you are there you feel like being here, when you are here you feel like going there. Even after thirty years of marriage, eight, nine children, people think "Did I do a mistake? Should I have taken a spiritual path?" Even after ten years in brahmacharya,[2] "Did I do a mistake?" There

---

1 Referring to the Isha Yoga Center, located at the foothills of the Velliangiri Mountains, Tamil Nadu, India.

2 The path of the divine. A life of celibacy and studentship on the path of spirituality, moving towards ultimate liberation.

are a few like that.

This is not today's problem; it is an age-old problem. Whatever you wish to do, you must bring yourself to a moment of joy and clarity within yourself, and at that moment what you decide – even if you die – you must go by that. Why I am saying joy is because when you are happy you are not compulsive. When you are very happy and clear, at that time if you look at things and see that "Yes, this is what is more sensible for me" – just do that. It does not matter if you go through hell for ten years, you just do that, because that is where your wellbeing is. Whenever your emotions go up and down, your mind says many things – that is not important. It says one thing in the morning, one thing in the evening; it says one thing today and another thing tomorrow, that is of no consequence. When you are in different states of compulsiveness, if you make decisions as to which way to turn, you will be endlessly lost.

Nischala Tatvam, Jeevan Mukti.[3] It is not about what you are doing. It is just that you are doing it in an unwavering way, you have become one pointed. It does not matter what it is – if you want to be a butcher, be a butcher in an unwavering way, it will open up. What you have decided in a moment of clarity and joy, just stick onto it, without wavering a little bit. Nobody can deny it to you. If every

3 A line from the Sanskrit composition "Bhaja Govindam," written by the eighth century Indian philosopher, Adi Shankaracharya. Lit. "from an unwavering, steady mind comes liberation in this life".

day you are off and on, off and on, it will not happen.

Every day when your thoughts and emotions fly this way and that, you keep changing your mind. Changing your mind, changing your mind, you will go endlessly in circles. One who changes direction too often is obviously not interested in going anywhere, isn't it? You know the world is round, so whichever direction you go, it does not matter; as long as you go without changing direction you will complete the journey. If you want to be there, be there, no problem. If you want to be here, be here. Don't go on changing your mind every day. Morning one way, evening another way – you are a torture to yourself and everyone around you. Right now you may be thinking, "Tomorrow morning, I am going to do my yoga." Tomorrow morning when the gong rings at five o'clock in the morning, your body says "To hell with this yoga, all I want to do is sleep." Its priorities keep changing.

There is another way to live where the greatest pleasures that you have known in your life will look like an ant's pleasure. This being is capable of that. When it comes to body and mind, we are all differently capable; no two bodies are equally capable, no two minds are equally capable. But when it comes to your being, every being is equally capable of containing the very existence within himself.

Scientists are saying, "It is ever-expanding, how to contain it?" That is the whole beauty of it. That which is endless, that which is eternal, that which is boundless, and that which is always expanding can be contained in this being.

It has not happened simply because you keep changing direction; wherever you find a little niche which is comfortable, you try to settle down there. This so-called "getting civilized" has become a huge detriment for spiritual process. Not essentially, but if you were a nomad... You know what nomad means? It means you are not mad. Who is not a nomad? One who is mad. One who is mad settles down; one who is not mad, moves on and on, does not settle down anywhere.

The moment we stop being nomadic, we get into a certain kind of madness of safety and security. Whether it is physical, psychological, or emotional, we are always looking for that niche, where we can settle down and sleep. And once you find a niche and it gets too sweet and comfortable, then you do not have the courage to step out and once again make the journey.

If all you are looking for is a picnic, then it is okay. If you want to try to climb the Seventh Hill,[4] if you climb a certain distance, your knees will be creaking and your breath will be sounding like a steam locomotive, "passshh, pussshh, passshh, pussshh." Then you look around; the beautiful rocks, the bamboo around you and the valley is so beautiful, everything is so wonderful. "What is the purpose of taking one more step?" Your mind tells you, "This is wonderful. This is it."

I am not questioning the beauty of the place; I am not

---

4 The seventh peak of the Velliangiri Mountains, it is considered to be a sacred site and is visited by thousands of pilgrims every year.

questioning the pleasure of being there. But right now this argument has come in you simply because your lungs are working like a steam engine, and your legs are creaking like an unoiled bullock cart.

Do you see every time, for different states of comfort or discomfort you get into, you develop a new logic? Have you noticed this with yourself? Like they say, when you are a student, everyone is a communist. The moment you come out of your education and get yourself a job, you become a socialist. The moment you get married, you become a capitalist. According to your new situations, new levels of logic will come. Now the world has come to a point where the Maoists have become capitalist, that is it!

It keeps happening. That is why in a certain moment of clarity and joy, when you look at something, what you see as your wellbeing, you stick to that. Tomorrow it looks like horror to you, it feels like hell, it does not matter, you stick to it. That is wellbeing.

Questioner: When I am truly joyful and clear, there is an exuberance inside; it is like I am melting. But people around me are pulling me down, even though I try not to let them. And if I keep to myself, I feel lonely. What should I do?

Sadhguru: I want you to understand this. The more lonely you feel, the more depressed you feel, the more the need for company. The more joyful you become, the more exuberant you become, and the less and less you need company. So if you feel lonely when you are alone, that means you are obviously in bad company! If you were with a good person why would you feel lonely? You would feel great. Exclusive. Now people's idea of exuberance is "Let's talk, let's dance, let's listen to music, let's do this, let's do that!" Not necessarily. You can just sit quietly here and be absolutely exuberant.

If your exuberance is manufactured, then you need company. If you are exuberant by your own nature, if life has become exuberant, activity is just a consequence. But if your life is not exuberant, and you are trying to crank it up with activity, then activity is the means.

This is the big difference. Either you dance and arrive at a certain state of exuberance, or because you are exuberant and you cannot contain it, you dance. These are two different things. Either because you are happy you burst out into laughter, or someone told you, "Every day in the morning if you laugh and laugh, one day you will become happy." These are two different ways. Look at everything around you; tell me, which way does life work?

Is it because there are flowers that the plant and the root came up like a support to the flower? Because there is a beautiful flower, this plant and its root grew, so that it can have a nice pedestal? Because the exuberance in the stem could not be contained, it flowered, isn't it? This is the way life should happen. If you try to live the other way, it is going to be a very hard life.

The hardest life in the world is to be constantly putting yourself out into the world like you are joyful when you are not. When you are not happy, to show everyone that you are happy, it costs phenomenal amount of life. Have you noticed this? There are some people who, when they are happy, they are happy; when they are not happy, they are not happy. They just show it to everyone, the whole world knows their act of life. Some people manage to pretend all the time, but it takes a phenomenal amount of energy to keep it up like that. You will grow diseases in your body, I am telling you. You will grow lumps and tumors in your body, if you constantly try to put on an act. This is happening all over the world.

Actually if you are willing to be a subject, I can demonstrate it to you; within a few hours I can make you grow a tumor. Really. If you make your mind in a certain way, you will do that to yourself. The only saving grace for you is that you never do anything steadily. Your joy is off and on, your misery is off and on, never fully on. If you become utterly miserable, you will see the consequence of it. If you become utterly joyful, you will see the consequence of it. If you become utterly angry, you will see the consequence of it. You do not see the consequence of anything because you are always off and on.

People ask me, "Sadhguru, what kind of attitude and emotion should I have?" I say, "Any damn thing is okay."

You want to be angry, be angry twenty-four hours, non-stop; you will get realized. I am not joking. If you like love, be loving twenty-four hours. You will get realized. Just keep it on for twenty-four hours, you will come to a certain realization. That is all it takes.

Everything, every cell, every atom in the existence can be a doorway to the beyond if you go steadily at it. But the problem is, people keep shifting and shifting. That is the biggest problem with today's world, like never before. People think it is a virtue for them to say, "Our attention spans are very short." If you keep shifting, nothing happens. Which way you want to go, I am not deciding that – go wherever you want to go, but steadily. Not every day altering it.

Questioner: Sadhguru, you were talking about perception and clarity, but at the same time, illusion also looks so very real. Where is that fine line between illusion and perception? How do I rationalize between "Okay, I am in an illusory state" or "I am in perfect clarity?" How do I really make that distinction at any given moment?

Sadhguru: Now you are talking about the line between illusion and perception. There is no fine line. It is all one big illusion. By the time you know it, life has passed by, but you do not have to worry, because passing by is also an illusion. Nothing passes by.

If everything is illusion, isn't enlightenment one big

illusion? In a way it is. That is why I have been talking, not about knowing, but about ignorance. In some of these programs,[5] earlier we used to make our brochures like this: "From ordinary to extraordinary. Do this yoga and you will move from ordinary to extraordinary." People thought they were going to become very special. After they came in, after they enrolled, paid their money, then we told them, "This is about becoming more ordinary than others, extra-ordinary this is not about becoming special."

The club of the enlightened ones is a place where there is no such thing as illusion and perception, where everything is illusion. Now you tell me, is number ten less of an illusion than number one? Is hundred more of a reality than number one? Everything is made up, isn't it so? The only reality is zero; the rest is all made up. It is not incidental that zero was discovered in India. This is the culture where the maximum number of people spent a huge amount of time with their eyes closed. If you sit with eyes closed, initially fantasies will go on, chattering will go on, gods will come, devils will come. If you simply sit, sit, sit, then you will see that you are one big vacuum. You are just one big zero.

If you perceive that you are an empty shell, would you call that perception, or would you call that a realization of what an illusion you are? It is up to you what you call it,

---

5 Referring to the Isha Yoga program, a scientific approach to spirituality offered by Isha. It is a method designed by Sadhguru that transmits powerful tools for individual transformation.

but there is no fine line, that is the whole problem. Or that is the beauty of it – there is no fine line, there are no lines to cross, it is just fine the way it is. But the problem is you are in a certain state of compulsiveness that you have to move somewhere.

This compulsiveness has essentially come as a consequence of the huge accumulation that you have made within yourself. This accumulation has happened because you have the illusion that you are perceiving something. You are actually not perceiving anything. Tell me, after all these years of being with me, what have you perceived? Whatever you perceived and you are feeling wonderful about, two days later I come back and demolish it anyway. Whatever you think you have attained, I come back and trample it anyway. So what have you perceived in these many years?

Slowly you are beginning to make yourself comfortable in your ignorance. That is good, because that is the only place you can be. And that is not some kind of damnation. That is the beauty and the mystery of life. In so many ways we told you in the Isha Yoga program itself, "You are nothing." Can "nothing" be perceived, or is it an illusion? Nothingness means non-existence. That means you are an illusion yourself; you are a make-believe happening. But you do not know. You think you are something.

When you say the illusion looks real, only illusion can look real. If you go to a cinema, you see people on the cinema screen, they are not even three-dimensional. All the great heroes that you have seen – and you may have joined the fan club, a Rajnikanth[6] club or Robert Redford[7] club, or whatever – all that you saw of them was just flat on the screen, just a little bit of light playing. If you raised your hand, the great hero's face would be gone and your hand would be there. That is how fragile he was, but didn't he look larger than life? Don't you worship him today more than all the people around you who are flesh and blood? You only saw light and sound. Though they are only two-dimensional, what happens in the cinema is much more real than the reality of life. Illusion is always exaggerated. It definitely looks more real than the real, always.

Have you heard of Ramakrishna Paramahamsa? Ramakrishna became a devotee of Kali.[8] For him, Kali was not a deity; Kali was a living reality. She danced in front of him, she ate from his own hands, she came when he called, and she left him dripping with ecstasy. This was real, it was actually happening – you could have tested him if you wanted; chemically, he was all ecstasy.

One day he was sitting on the banks of the Hoogli River,

---

6 A popular Indian film actor, nicknamed "Superstar." He started his life as a bus conductor in Bangalore and with his distinct stylishness and flair, he rose to become a phenomenal icon in Tamil Nadu.

7 Californian actor and movie director who has received two Oscars. Founder of the acclaimed Sun-dance film festival.

8 A powerful goddess, a fierce depiction of the feminine energy, signifying annihilation.

and a very great yogi, a rare yogi – very few like that have ever happened – Totapuri came this way. Though Ramakrishna's body, mind and emotion were dripping with ecstasy, his being was longing to go beyond this ecstasy. Because somewhere there was an awareness that that itself is a bondage.

When I tell people simple things about their lives, when I say everyone has the choice right now to be either this way or that way, people say, "That is easy for you, Sadhguru, you are aware." Tell me, who is not aware? Please look at yourself and see. Even in an extreme moment of emotion or anger, there is a spot of awareness even in you. If it is not there, that means you have become pathologically ill. Otherwise, even in the most extreme moments of emotion within you, there is one dot of awareness. It is just that you are empowering the emotion because you have an investment there, but you are not empowering the awareness, that is all. Have you ever had a situation in your life when there was not even a spot of awareness in you? It was always there. It is just that you did not invest on that. You are betting on the wrong horse. You are betting on the horse that you are used to, a known horse.

Because of your friendship with your anger, friendship with your love, friendship with pleasure, friendship with whatever sweet emotions that can happen within you, you are investing on that.

So Ramakrishna was longing somewhere, but the sweet-ness of ecstasy that he was experiencing was too much to leave and go. This should not be misunderstood, but this is not any different from a drunkard being addicted to his drink, a drug addict being addicted to some substance. The only thing that is different is alcohol and drug may be damaging the system. This may not be damaging the system because this is internal, but the addiction is same, the attachment is same, the longing for that is same and the limitation is also same.

It is beautiful; there is no question about that. Ramakrishna, whenever he had contact with Kali, his object of devotion, he would be dripping with ecstasy, and he was fine with that. He did not want to leave the beauty of that and move on.

When Totapuri came, this transpired between them...

Totapuri said, "This is very simple. You have the necessary energy, you just have to empower your awareness. You are empowering your emotion, you are empowering your body, you are empowering the chemistry within you. You are not empowering your awareness."

Ramakrishna said, "Okay, I will empower my awareness and sit like this."

The moment he has a vision of Kali, he is again gone into uncontrollable states of love and ecstasy. Any number of times he sat down, but the moment he sees Kali, he just flies off.

Then Totapuri said, "Next time Kali appears, you have to take a sword and cut her into pieces."

Ramakrishna asked, "Where do I get the sword from?"

Totapuri said, "From the same place where you get Kali. If you are able to create a whole Kali, why can't you create a sword? You can do it. If you are able to create a goddess, why can't you create a sword to cut her? Get ready."

Ramakrishna sat down, and the moment Kali came, he burst into ecstasy and forgot about the sword and the awareness and everything.

Totapuri told him, "You sit this time, the moment Kali comes... see, here," he picked up a piece of glass, and he said, "With this piece of glass, I am going to cut you. Where you are stuck – that I am going to cut. When I cut that, you create the sword and cut Kali down."

When Ramakrishna was just on the edge of ecstasy, when Kali appeared in his vision, Totapuri took a piece of glass and cut him really deep across his forehead. Then Ramakrishna created the sword and cut Kali down, and he became free from the Mother and the ecstasy of feeding off her. And that is when he truly became a Paramahamsa. Until then, he was a lover, he was a devotee, he was a child to the Mother Goddess that he created.

This is not something that you go about making a distinction between what is reality and what is illusion. You don't do that. Whatever is happening within you, it does not matter what is happening within you, you keep your steering wheel straight. As I have been telling you for some time now, you keep your direction straight, whatever is happening within you, it does not matter, you just gas it and gas it and gas it. As long as you are travelling straight, you just keep the throttle down. Don't go off the gas pedal, just down and down and down. That is all. That is your business; rest I will take care. Your business is to put your right foot down, not the other one, just the right foot down all the time.

If you put your left foot down, it may touch the brakes or the clutch. Then you will simply rev in the same place; you will not go anywhere. All the time, a leaden foot down. Whatever is happening – illusion is happening, gas it; reality is happening, gas it. God is happening, gas it; Devil is happening, gas it. You have to break through all of that. You don't think, "Okay, this is reality, let me settle down here. This is illusion, let me discard this." No. You just gas your way through all that, it does not matter. You don't try to decipher what is illusion, what is reality. The moment you try to do that, it will become endless intellectual circus. It will lead to a purposeless circus, because it will not get you anywhere. It will make you look smart among people, but Existence will see you as stupid, because it does not open its doors for you. It does not matter how smart you are with people, how smart you are in the society, this Existence will not open its doors. It will open its doors only to the smartest, and the smartest is also the dumbest. Really.

"So shall I be dumb?" You cannot be dumb, just see that. If you try to be dumb, you are trying to be smart, isn't it? You are being super-smart. Do you see you cannot try to be stupid? If you are acting stupid, that means you are trying to be smart. That is why I always say, "Whatever is happening, see that you are stupid," because you cannot try to be stupid. You cannot do nothingness, isn't it? You can do something, you cannot do nothingness. You can be a somebody, but you cannot be a nobody. "I am a nobody" is a great assertion of your somebody-ness, isn't it? You cannot do it. When you tire and simply sit quietly, it happens. Your effort has to tire, or you need phenomenal intelligence to go beyond effort.

Right now, whatever is happening, you are only trying to get out of it. You are driving through the mountain, you are trying to get out of it. You are driving through wonderful plains, you are hurrying up to get out of it. All the time gas pedal down. Wherever you are, however beautiful it is, as quickly as possible you want to get out of it, that should be your intention always. However wonderful it is – you are in God's lap, you must be getting out of it as quickly as possible. If you are doing that constantly, then you will get to that ultimate stupidity, where you do not have to try to be smart – you have given up on that. Then you are at ease. Life is at ease. When this life that you call as "myself" comes to absolute ease, then the whole Existence is wide open, no door is closed, everything is open. Just everything – creation and Creator is accessible to you, simply because this has come to total ease.

Sadhguru

THE TRAP OF A DREAM

"A dream is more impactful than reality for most people."

Riding on the solidity of scientific theories and proven facts, one tries to go through life logically figuring everything out. Yet, amidst the logical structure of life, a few moments may come when one begins to wonder about what is beyond this enclosure.

What is the nature of the trap? How to recognize it? And how to become free? Step by step, Sadhguru takes the seeker by the hand, illuminating the suffocating trap and pointing the way out. Addressing the residents of the Isha Yoga Center in India, he gently fans that burning universal longing for freedom.

A seed of any kind in the world can find its ultimate potential through simple nourishment. A mango tree, if it finds soil and nourishment, will find its sweetness. A mango tree does not need a Guru to produce sweetness. When this is so, why is it that a human being, who seems to be the highest potential of all life on this planet, is not able to get to his Ultimate nature by himself? What is this trap? What is the nature of this trap? Why is outside help needed? Why can it not be an inside job?

It is just like, if you were trapped in a prison, if you were imprisoned, the prison is made in such a way that it does not provide tools to break through. Everything that could help you break through has been taken away in some way. If it has to be an inside job, then all the prisoners, or at least a substantial number of prisoners, should get together and push the gates or the walls or whatever. But if an individual prisoner makes an attempt to get out all by himself, the chances of him getting out of the prison are quite remote. Most prisoners who have been sentenced to life, though there is much longing to get out, never make it out because they do not have outside help. If you can organize all the prisoners together you could force your way out, but the very nature of these prisoners is such, it is very rare that they get organized.

Whether it is in the prison or in an ashram, all of them getting organized and functioning like one organism is rare. So, outside help from someone who is not in the same limitations, who is not imprisoned within himself and contained by the physical cage which is the body, someone who is free – that kind of help becomes inevitable and necessary. This is the reason why the wise traditions, particularly of the East, have always insisted on an enlightened Guru; or if he passes on, a strong *sangha*[9] or a *sathsang*, where people are together as one. Every realized being, before he left, always tried to organize his people into one group. Those who did not do it, the moment they left, the very spiritual process lost its relevance. When the master was there, it worked. The moment he was gone, the very spiritual process became irrelevant because they did not organize a strong organism of people. When the Guru is alive, the sangha is not so important, but when he is alive if the necessary organization is not done, it is impossible to put people together after he is gone.

You are trapped in this mechanism that you call as "myself," which is self-created – because who you are right now is just a memory of the past. Everything that you are right now is just a memory. Both memory and imagination have no existential relevance; they are not true. It is for this reason that for ages they went on insisting that everything you are experiencing right now – your very life and existence as an individual – is a dream, it is *maya*, it is an illusion.

"If it is maya, why do I suffer? Right now, my body is aching, is that maya? My knees are hurting, is this maya?"

---

9 A group or congregation of spiritual seekers.

You must understand this: whatever you believe becomes your reality.

If you walk into the forest at night, and if you fear snakes, if you just see a dead tree branch lying there, you think it is a king cobra. A branch looks like that usually. In the moonlight, it looks like a king cobra, and then someone behind you sighed – some people are always sighing – now you think the snake is hissing too. The moment you think it is a snake, your whole body reacts to that. You start sweating, getting paralyzed, fearful, everything that needs to happen with a snake happens just because you believe it is so. There is no such thing there. It does not matter, but you believe it is so. That is the way it works for you.

Let us say you are walking in the forest, and there really is a king cobra with his hood raised, standing up six feet tall – a king cobra can stand up to six-and-a-half to seven feet tall – he is looking at you like dinner, but you do not know. It is too dark, you cannot see it. Everything will be just fine with you, like a picnic, because you believe it is safe.

The very nature of how you are made right now is whatever you believe becomes your reality. This complex, huge heap of impressions of memory that have been taken in, which have been manipulated into different shapes and forms according to your thought and emotion, has become such a complex prison. Figuring your way through the prison is not possible, because who you are is controlled by it. You built a prison, and this was not built with the intention of imprisoning yourself, but with the intention of self-preservation. The walls that you build for self-preservation are also the walls of self-imprisonment. It just takes a little while to realize that.

Once you build this wall with a complex amalgamation of memory, imagination and emotion, your very software is such that it is not geared to cross this wall. You are not even going and knocking your head on the wall because your software is geared only to run within the walls, never to even go and touch the wall. Unless you become conscious enough of those dimensions of memory which are on the unconscious levels of your memory bank, unless you move to that space, you will not even touch the wall. Your software keeps you well within the wall space, never even making an attempt.

Within the prison, you will seek freedom, you seek power. You know, inside the prisons somebody runs a whole kingdom. He is the boss there, he manages things there, he feels like a king inside a prison. Within the prison you can seek a certain amount of power and freedom, that is allowed, but if you become powerful within the prison, you will not even make an attempt to get out of the prison. Such a longing will not come. Prisoners who are convicted in a prison for a short-term sentence do not get involved with all this – they are just eager to get out. Those who are there for life, they know there is no way out of it, so they form kingdoms inside. They know they are anyway going to be inside the prison for the rest of their life, so they are trying to make something out of it, find some kind of meaning to an imprisoned life. Outside help unfortunately becomes necessary because without it you will not even realize there is another possibility. Generally, most prisons in the world are very orderly, they are kept well. Everyone gets up on time, goes to bed on time, eats on time, everything happens on time. It is a very orderly arrangement because for the people who manage the prison, this order is the safety. If there is a disorderly moment, they cannot figure out what is happening there. But a prison which is very orderly is very hard to escape from.

If you get very organized within yourself, you will see that the prison becomes very hard to break. A very orderly prison is always a secure prison. The more secure a prison is, the farther away from freedom you are. It needs a little chaos. When things are chaotic, it is easier to break through the walls. But if chaos goes beyond a point, it becomes unmanageable. To maintain a balance of a certain order and a certain level of chaos is a lot of complex management.

Once it happened, a surgeon, a general and a politician, all of them retired, met in the coffee shop of a golf club. The surgeon did not have his scalpel, the general did not have his guns, the politician did not have his power or his people. They were just talking and the surgeon said, "Of all the professions in the world, my profession of being a surgeon is the oldest profession."

The other two asked, "How so?"

He said, "Before Adam and Eve, it was just Adam and one of Adam's ribs was taken out. From that rib, Eve was made. Who else but a great surgeon can do that? So, it is the oldest profession."

The general said, "No, no, no, you are missing one point. Before even Adam came, do you remember, it says that there was chaos, and order was brought? Who else but a good soldier can bring order to such a situation? The soldier's job was the first thing in this creation."

The politician chuckled and said, "All that is fine, but who created that chaos?"

Managing chaos just enough so that your system does not get too orderly, and the prison does not become too strong that it cannot be broken, can only be done by someone who is not in the prison. One who is in the prison cannot do that; if he creates chaos, he will create totally destructive chaos. Only someone who is not sentenced can create such a thing.

It is because of this that traditions always insisted on a live Guru, and where the situations were conducive, these Gurus demanded total surrender. Where it was not conducive, they talked elaborate philosophies. Krishna very unabashedly said, "You have to surrender to me, there is no other way." He never feared, it never occurred to him that someone may think he is too egoistic. Saying "I am everything, you must surrender to me" is a very dangerous statement in today's world. But he never felt like that. He lived in a situation where he could simply say this. In recent times we have not had freedom to say such things. You have to weave it around and weave it around before you ever bring people to such a state.

Here in this culture, people have been trained to surrender. Right from their childhood, wherever you take your children, children are told, "First thing is bow down. Any elderly person you see, first bow down, touch their feet." This is because the whole culture, the whole nation at one time lived with a single-minded purpose of Ultimate liberation. The whole population in this land was completely dedicated to Ultimate liberation. Mukti was the only goal in their life. Because of that, the culture trained people right from their childhood not to make too much out of yourself. Just bow down to everything that you see.

Like this, many devices were built so that surrender becomes natural, but then we got English educated, and it became very difficult to bow down. In the West, it was always taught to people, "Never bow down to anybody. You stand up straight. Never bow down," because bowing down was seen as a weakness. Surrender is unthinkable. The most horrible thing that you can do is surrender. They never realized the beauty of surrender.

From falling in love, they have twisted themselves out to making love. Falling became a negative thing; surrender and bowing down became negative things. By doing this, humanity has surrendered the most beautiful aspect within a human being, they have surrendered the beauty of life to gross ego. Ego is worshipped. The very idea that you need someone to come out of your limitations has become unacceptable. With that, it may take an extremely long time to even realize that there is a possibility beyond the way you exist right now.

If one celebrates their ego as strength, if one does not understand the limitations of his existence and believes oneself to be everything, or if one is unwilling to be helped because it is considered weakness, then to even realize there is a possibility will take a very long time. If a different type of sense, which is not of the five senses, has to arise within you, first of all, you must understand the limitations of the five senses.

Once, a young wife was sharing with a friend, "It looks like my husband has a sixth sense."

Her friend asked, "How so? How do you know this?"

She said, "Because, it is obvious he doesn't have the five. So he must have a sixth sense."

If you simply sit with me, just the presence of what is here, suddenly something is struggling to go beyond the physical. That makes some people noisy, some people very mobile, some people like mopping machines on the floor. Different expressions, but essentially what is happening is that something beyond the physical does not like the physical limitations. But even for this to happen, I want you to understand, it has happened with outside help. Otherwise, this life would have gone on, without ever knowing anything like that. Just ideas and stories. Ideas and stories are not transformation; they just create a dream, and a dream is more real than reality.

Suppose you were fast asleep and dreaming, and you thought an elephant has come into your bedroom. You got terrified, and out of that fear you woke up, and there is no elephant. Even though there is no elephant, you will still sweat, you will palpitate, you will go through everything as if something happened. The moment you woke up, you know it was just a dream, but still you fear.

When we say a dream, don't take it lightly – a dream is more impactful than reality for most people. The trap of a dream is not a simple trap. It is a very powerful trap that is self-created. Especially because it is self-created, you have no means to break it. There is a certain sense of attachment and liking for what you have created. You cannot break it. Have you seen at different stages in your life, some silly little things which are in your drawer, you know it is of no use, but you cannot throw it away? Even if it is causing some trouble, you cannot throw it away because it has been there for so long. There is a certain sense of attachment to it.

It is very hard to break what you create. It takes clarity of perception or it needs outside help. Otherwise it could take a very long time. And when I say "long time," I am not talking in terms of years... it could take a very, very long time.

Asking for outside help, or even if it comes unasked, to allow outside help, needs a certain gracefulness and humility. Otherwise, you cannot allow outside help. Lots of people cannot receive something gracefully. Always, the social ethics have taught you that giving is important, taking is not important. Yes, taking is not important, taking is ugly, but receiving is very important.

Actually, you are receiving everything that is worthwhile in your life. I want you to just look at any aspect of it. Right now, the clothes that you are wearing, for this cloth to sit on you right now, do you know how many things and how many people are involved in delivering this? Someone planted a cotton seed; then that plant grew up – a million organisms were involved in making this plant grow up; and then the whole process from ginning, to spinning, to weaving – do you know how many people it takes? Then the cloth, the maker, the seller, the agent, and everyone else, and now here it is, sitting on you. How many thousands of people are involved in just this cloth sitting on your body right now! The food that you ate, for it to get into your system, how many people and how many different lives have participated in making this happen? None of these things you could do all by yourself.

If you understand this and receive this gracefully, you will be overwhelmed with gratitude. If gratitude becomes your very life breath, you will also become very receptive. When you are grateful, you are very receptive. Not a cultivated gratitude; people have always told you the three magic words – one of them is "Thank you." Gratitude happens to you when you are overwhelmed by something or someone. Suppose you were very hungry and you thought you were going to die. If someone just gave you a piece of bread, now tears of gratitude would come to you. If they gave you a loaf at some other time when you were well, it would not have meant anything to you. But at that moment, when you look at that person who gave you the piece of bread, there is enormous gratitude because you are overwhelmed by the experience.

With every aspect of your life – a piece of cloth, a piece of bread, or a morsel of food, what it takes for it to be created and to land on your plate and get into your body – if you recognize how much is involved to make a single aspect of your life happen, gratitude happens. If you just see, from microorganisms to human beings, how many lives are participating in making things happen for you every moment of your life, if you are conscious of it, if you peel your eyes and look at it properly, you will be overwhelmed with gratitude because you could never do this by yourself.

Gratitude is also a state of surrender, please see this. When you are grateful, you very naturally bow down. No one has to tell you. I do not know if you have noticed this, even if someone does not belong to Eastern cultures, even if bowing down is not at all a part of their culture, when they are grateful, they will stand a little bent. Have you noticed this? They will not stand erect. When they are full of gratitude, there is a need to bow down. Being over-whelmed with gratitude and surrender are not different. Instead of surrender, we could talk the language of gratitude, because it still accommodates your ego a little bit. Surrender is too pure. Too pure, in that, there is no room for any of your nonsense. In gratitude, you can still be there a little bit. If gratitude happens as step one, surrender will naturally follow.

Questioner: Sadhguru, when I'm at the height of my emotions, surrender seems to be the nearest, sweetest thing possible. When so many other things overpower me, it goes out of my vision. Can I consciously do the Sharanagati?[10]

Sadhguru: Don't try to surrender because what is it that you are going to surrender? If you bend down, that is not surrender, that is good exercise. If you declare, "I have surrendered," that is a horrible ego. How will you surrender? What have you got to surrender first of all? It is out of a certain realization that surrender happens.

These words can be very misleading because you have always been taught self-worth, self-esteem, confidence – these are the valuable things that make your life. Surrender is against all of these. Only when you are worthless, you can surrender. If you have self-worth, self-esteem, confidence, how to surrender? But can you live without confidence, self-esteem, or some sense of self-worth? Right now, no.

I have no sense of self-esteem or self-worth. That is why, if necessary, the next moment I am willing to go, because

10 Lit. surrender in Sanskrit.

personally I do not think this is worth anything, keeping this on. But because it seems to be useful for many lives around us, we keep this going. But there is no self-worth, because the sense of self itself is gone, so where can there be worth?

Self is not worth anything, and to that which is not worth anything if you add esteem, that is a lot of trouble. And because of this esteem, if this worthless thing becomes confident, that is real trouble. But for the sake of survival, people believed unless you believe in yourself you cannot survive. It is not true in an essential way, but people believe that, and it becomes true for them. Whatever you believe in, if you add sufficient focus and emotion to it, it becomes very real.

All kinds of nonsensical belief systems around the world have become absolutely real for lots of people. For a vast majority of population, it has become real. They believe it, and it is so. But whatever you believe and whatever you empower with your thoughts and your emotions have no existential basis.

When you talk surrender, you are talking about passing from the limitations of one dimension to another. You knocked your head on the wall sufficiently, now you understood that unless you become like thin air, you will not pass. Suppose you are imprisoned and the doors are thick; you cannot escape. There is a filthy gutter; if you crawl through this filth, you can get out to freedom. Will you choose to crawl through the filth or not? If that is the only route to freedom, through the most horrible filth, you will crawl. It will go into your nostrils, your mouth and everywhere, but it does not matter. That is surrender because you have realized that you cannot cross the prison walls standing, so you are crawling.

Surrender is a certain realization that in your present form you cannot pass the gate. So you find a more intelligent way to pass. That will not come by cultivation, but only by a certain realization. And this comes either out of your intelligence, or because life has ground you sufficiently. Or because you are insane enough to fall in love in an unbridled way – not in a conditional, sensible or nice way – in an insane way. Insane like a Ramakrishna, or a Mirabai,[11] or Akka Mahadevi.[12] There have been any number of them who are insane; these are the known names. They are not sane, they are not at all nice, but they are fantastic. That which is fantastic need not be nice. Usually, it is not nice. I am not nice either.

Questioner: Sadhguru, the world is shrinking because of communication. Should we welcome other cultures or should we stick to our own culture? If we welcome other cultures, then to what extent?

---

11 A Rajput princess of the medieval period in India who, intoxicated by her devotion for Lord Krishna, spent most of her life as a wandering saint, singing praises of her Lord.

12 A 12th century Indian saint. She was a queen in the state of Karnataka who left the palace to go in search for Shiva, whom she considered her husband. Her spiritual couplets are revered even today as classical poetry.

Sadhguru: The world is shrinking because of communication? Yes, definitely we can reach across the world with a simple gadget like a cell phone. In terms of our ability to communicate and travel, it is true; we can go around the world in twenty-four hours' time. In that way, yes, but in terms of human relationship and experience, the world is not shrinking, the world is going apart in a big way. Like never before, humanity is suffering from loneliness. If it was shrinking, if truly communication was happening, there should have been no such thing as loneliness. Today, it is a very common sight to see husband and wife walking together, both of them talking on the cell phone to someone else. Don't you see that all over the place? They are together!

Those who are far have become near, those who are near have become far because of electronic communication. People are in your house, but they are watching the television. Are they with you? They are somewhere else. They are playing cricket in Kolkata. Nobody is with you. I am not speaking against it. It is just that I do not think the world is shrinking, it is reorganizing itself because of communication technology.

Because there is a television in your house, what is happening anywhere in the world is happening in your house. All kinds of people, the kinds you would have never allowed into your house, have all entered. Murderers, drunkards, drug addicts, rapists, everybody is entering your house now. Once you turn on the television, who comes and who does not come is not your choice. Everybody comes into your house. "How much of it should I allow? Should I allow it or not? Should I stick to my own culture or should I welcome other cultures? Should I integrate culture or resist the influence of other cultures?"

The first thing I want you to understand is, generally what you call as culture is what somebody did yesterday; the mess they created yesterday is today's culture. The mess that you create today is tomorrow's culture. Cultures were generally not engineered towards a purpose. They generally happened according to the requirements of the land, the time, and the situation that existed at that time. A few cultures were engineered in a certain way, but generally, most of the cultures just happened because of the events they faced.

"Should I stick to my culture or someone else's culture?" Every culture has something to offer. If you have chosen to take your life in a particular direction, a certain type of culture may be suitable. If you have chosen to take your life in a different direction, another kind of culture is suitable. If you have chosen to be on the spiritual path, then you need to create a certain type of culture.

Wherever there was genuine spiritual process, uncannily you will see they generally developed the same kinds of cultures. If there was a realized being and he spoke about how to be, you will see it is almost word by word the same anywhere. But over a period of time, those things get distorted, get influenced by the local cultures and organized forms of religion, and get into a totally different shape and form.

At one time, a long time ago, the whole subcontinent of India had a culture like what we are trying to create here in Isha[13] – a very well-balanced state of chaos and order. It is very difficult to manage these two things at the same time. If we want to make everything orderly, it is very easy. Everything will work properly, but spirit will die. If you make it very chaotic, people will become very spirited, but things will collapse. Once things collapse, people also fall apart.

It is like a rollercoaster. When we say a rollercoaster, people usually think it is a wild thing. Not true. A rollercoaster is more controlled than your car. If you drive your car, it may go off here and there a little bit; any moment you can go off the road and back on the road. A rollercoaster is 100% fixed on its rails, always on the track, never going off for a moment. Perfect order, but on the surface it is total disorder. Only the people sitting in it think it is a wild thing. The people who are managing it think it is a perfect machine, in proper order. It never goes off the track.

We are trying to manage it like a rollercoaster. One part of it is always perfectly on rails. The rest of it is going wild. It looks like you do not want to have anything to do with it because it is so crazy. At the same time, the bottom line is fixed so perfectly well that it never goes off the track. It takes a steady stomach to take that ride.

---

13 Lit: Formless Divine energy. Here referring to the non-profit organization, Isha Foundation, created by Sadhguru to offer a spiritual possibility to the world.

Don't choose any cultures. Act intelligently in your life, without identifying with any culture. If you are choosing to go in a particular direction, a certain type of culture is advantageous. If your life is all about enjoying the physicality of life, turn West. They do it better. If your life is about knowing the inner dimensions, turn East. We have always done it better. The choice is not about which culture. The choice is, what is it that you want to do with your life? What is suitable for your way, your search, your longing? You arrange your life intelligently around that; you will belong to some culture. What does it matter?

When I was just four or five years of age, my parents were not such temple-going people. Though they had no such inclination, somehow their culture told them to go, and they wanted to go to the temple once in two, three months. When they want to go to the temple, I have questions. I had a condition, "If you cannot answer the question, I am not entering the temple." They could not answer my questions, so I never entered the temple. So where to leave me? They always left me with the footwear man and they gave him some money.

If they had given me that money, I would have sat in one place! They don't understand the dynamics of life. Because since I was nine, ten years of age, I earned my own pocket money, always. I never took a single rupee from my parents. Even when I was four or five, I understood the dynamics well. If they had given me the money, "This is the fee for you staying quiet," I would have just stayed quiet. Instead of that, they gave the money to that footwear man and told him, "You make sure that he stays right here... and he is not easy." I remember he would do his business with one hand. With the other hand, he always held me. So, there was no escape.

I sat there and I was trying to understand his business. People came and they left their footwear with him. At that time, it was just five paise per pair, or ten paise if you have a family or something. Then, someone would want to save some money and they would leave their footwear elsewhere, without leaving it with him. Sometimes, these outside footwear, God puts it on and walks away! When these people come out, and see their footwear is missing, they curse the creation and the Creator. Sometimes they think this man has engineered this footwear disappearance and a whole drama happens. And even this man did not keep footwear in a proper way. Whatever he collected, he threw it in a heap and when people came, he gave them the wrong footwear – a whole drama was happening.

This footwear thing went deep into me. So, when we first started doing the yoga programs, the first thing I said was, "Footwear should be parked properly." Wherever you go, Isha Yoga means, footwear will be neatly parked outside. No confusion about it and we do not let God walk away with it.

You bring this culture into yourself, whether it is footwear or a crown, you handle it with the same care, and concern. Whether it is an ant or an elephant, you treat it with the same concern. Whether someone is a king or a beggar, you treat them the same way within yourself. You learn to do the simple tasks of your life and the most important tasks of your life with the same involvement. Whatever you have seen in the Isha Yoga programs, the volunteers are going about as if carpets are some kind of precision instruments. Have you seen this? They are going on stretching them like this, holding it like this, holding it like that – it must be placed exactly where it should be. Yes, everything in your life must be handled that way.

Here in Isha, everyone is a volunteer. A volunteer simply means someone who is willing. Not willing to do just this or that, someone who is willing to do just anything. If you do not make a distinction whether something is small or big, if you do not make a distinction whether something is dear to you or not dear to you, if you handle everything with the same level of involvement, that is a good culture. That is a very good, conducive culture for a spiritual seeker. No other culture is good for you. That should be your culture – a culture of involvement with everything.

These are two types of cultures: everything is important or nothing is important. These two are spiritual in nature. There are some people who do not care for anything. There are some people who are concerned about everything. But the moment you think that something is important and something else is not important, you are on the wrong culture. This is great, this is not great, this is good, this is bad – the moment you make this distinction and start treating things accordingly within yourself, you are on the wrong culture.

There is some discretion in how we handle things outside;

but within you, there is no discretion, everything is same. If you just learn this and put this into your life, you are on the right culture. That is not spirituality; it creates a conducive atmosphere for a spiritual process.

This is the reason why in the Eastern cultures, if you see a cow, you bow down. If you see a snake, you bow down, if you see a tree, you bow down. If you see a beggar, you bow down, if you see a king, you bow down; if you see God, you bow down. Whatever you see, you bow down. This is not some kind of subservience. This is taking away the distinction of your judgment as to what is important and what is not important. Everything that has been created in this existence is important. That is why it is here.

If the Creator thought it is worthwhile to create a rock, why do you think it is not important? If the Creator took such elaborate care to create an ant – have you looked at an ant closely? You will see, it is an exquisite piece of art. If someone took so much care to create this tiny little creature, who the hell are you to think it is not important?

If you can look upon and act upon everything in your life with the same sense of involvement, that is the best culture. You must bring that culture into yourself and your children. It will do good, wherever they go, East or West.

Questioner: *Sadhguru, I see what you are saying, but how can I bring that culture into myself, where I'm open to everything?*

Sadhguru: When we did the ninety-day Wholeness program,[14] though I was using logic, we were slowly taking them into a realm that they could never logically understand. For ninety days, people just stayed in the ashram – and there was no ashram, it was just a hut. They just stayed there. This was the first program that happened there. We made them see things that they had never believed possible.

As the program was going on, I would ask a question and they would say, "That was okay, but this, Sadhguru..." And I would keep asking, "Yes or no, yes or no, yes or no?" The first few days and weeks there was this struggle, but as their experiences went into a completely different realm, all of them developed one slogan. When I walked into the hall one day, they wrote on a huge banner: "Yes and yes." Whatever you ask, before you ask the question – "yes and yes."

If you become "yes and yes" to life, everything will happen beautifully, nobody can stop it. Being a volunteer means training yourself to become "yes and yes." "Oh, is this being stupid? Can't I use my discretionary mind?" If you used your discretionary mind to its fullest extent, you would naturally become "yes and yes." Because you have used it in immature ways, you have become "no and no" or "no, no, no, no, no... oh, yes."

A lot of people in India, when they speak the English

---

14 Program conducted in 1994, where Sadhguru led a group of forty seekers on an intense inward journey, through powerful spiritual practices.

language, they say, "no, no, no, no, no, no, no." Have you heard this? I keep reminding people, "Just one is enough." If you say, "yes, yes, yes," okay. We want to hear that. When you say "no," one is enough, isn't it? It is not just a way of speaking – people have become one big "no." To get them to say "yes," it needs coaxing, you have to woo them, otherwise they will not say yes.

If you do not want to say yes, learn to say neither. Not in conversations – with life. If you can simply be like this: no "yes," no "no" – then the problem is, you will become an ascetic. People think an ascetic is a no to the world. He is neither yes nor no. "Whatever life is, let it be." That is one big yes, isn't it? That is another way of saying yes, without uttering it.

If whichever way life is, that is the way you are, then you are one big yes, because life is all yes. Everything is transacting with everything, it is just one big yes. If the tree says, "No. Why should these idiots breathe the oxygen that I give out? I will hold back," for sure, he will die. You may not die. You will run to the next tree, you can go to the next garden, but he will die for sure.

If I say "no" to you, it is not that you will die, it is me who will die. "No" is the poison of life. If you drink the poison, you die, not someone else. But always, human beings have this idea of performing a miracle. When you become angry, resentful, fearful and hateful, you become no. But the problem is, whenever you become like this, whenever you become resentful, you think something will happen to someone. You drink the poison, but you expect somebody else to die. Life does not work like that. You drink it, you die.

The process of what we do here is to slowly make you into a "yes" – one big "yes." It is not that something is important, something is not important: everything is important. Whether it is about the program, or the kriya, or the volunteering process, all these things are structured so that you become "yes" in the body, "yes" in the mind, "yes" in your emotions and "yes" in your energy. It is very important, because all of them can self-imprison themselves; all of them are capable of that.

Questioner: Guruji, when you are in deep states of grief or pain, what can one do at that time to alleviate the suffering?

Sadhguru: Don't alleviate it, go deeper into it, because pain is one of the few things that you have which takes you very deep into yourself. Don't waste that opportunity. Just sink into it totally, succumb to it. It will take you very deep. If you can just maintain a certain awareness about it, then pain can be a tremendous tool of growth. Anyway you are suffering, why don't you use it for your growth, rather than try to apply a balm and get out of it? Once you have gone to a certain depth, you will not come out of it because somebody applies an ointment on you or says sweet words to you. Anytime tomorrow you will again fall back. Instead of that, consciously dig deeper into your pain, maintain a certain awareness about it; you will see pain becomes a tremendous rejuvenation and a tremendous rebirth for you.

If you are feeling painful, you come to me; I will make it more painful for you, because I do not think it is wrong. As long as people are growing, I do not care how they do it. Somehow you do it – Yogaratova, Bhogaratova[15] – somehow you do it. What does it matter how?

Questioner: Sadhguru, how should one prepare for the last leg of the journey on this planet, spiritually, physically, and morally?

Sadhguru: The last mile. A young boy and a girl who were studying in a college fell in love with each other. They fell in love and things built up. Problems of caste and creed came up for the family and the family said, "No way are you going any further with this. Enough loving you have done, leave it."

They said, "No, no we want to go ahead."

Big resistance and heat picked up. If the families don't create this heat, most love affairs will fall apart, really. If no one resists a love affair, they will leave it very easily. The moment they resist it, it becomes like a cause, like

---

15 A phrase from "Bhaja Govindam" which means to somehow attain to the Ultimate, whether through yoga or through bhoga (pleasure or enjoyment) – whichever way.

they are fighting an injustice. It went on and a big social thing happened. Then they decided, "This is it, we will end our lives." Their last leg on the planet. They came to Velliangiri hills.[16] There is a nice peak, if you climb up there, you have a clear 700–800 foot drop. Without touching anything, you can go for a free fall of that much at least.

They came there and said, "Let's jump."

The girl said, "Raju, I am feeling scared."

The boy was in the mood and said, "Come, hold my hand and jump."

She said, "No, you do it first, then I will come. I will be right behind you."

The boy had seen too many Hindi films and he jumped. The girl stood at the edge of the cliff and screamed, "Oh Raju, I love you!" Then the next level of logic came and she thought, "Oh, how sad. Raju is dead, but the problem is also over. All this family, society, all this clash is over. Why waste one more life?"

How should you do the last leg? Hurtling, free-falling. Because it is a last step, don't walk slowly, go all out. If you jump off a mountain or an airplane, you will fall. But that is the most beautiful thing that can happen to you, falling. Only problem is that the damn planet is waiting

16 Lit. White Mountains, these revered mountains are part of the Nilgiris Biosphere 30 kms from the city of Coimbatore, in South India. Known to be the abode of many sages and saints, Isha Yoga Center is located at their foothills.

there to receive you, otherwise the falling is an absolutely wonderful, miraculous experience.

Once it happened, Shankaran Pillai fell off the second floor and hurt himself. People gathered around him and asked, "Did the fall hurt you?"

He said, "You idiots, it is not the fall, it is the stopping."

So do not make a distinction between the first step and the last step. If you made a distinction in the beginning, and now you are towards the last steps, at least now you must learn. It does not matter whether you have another hundred steps to walk or just one – walk the same way, don't make the distinction. People say, "At least towards the end of your life, you must think about God." If you have lived your life so blindly that you did not look at anything, and the last moment you say, "Ram, Ram," and think everything will be okay, no, it does not work like that.

Have you heard of Biju Patnaik?[17] That man lived in his own way, quite freaky. On top of that, he was a Chief Minister, in political focus. When he was on his death bed, at that moment, people brought the Gita and they wanted to read it to him. He said, "Shut up with all that nonsense. I have lived my life well."

Usually, it does not matter if somebody was an atheist, when they are beginning to go they will think, "Maybe it

---

17 Started as a freedom fighter and later became a dynamic Indian politician. He was instrumental in Indonesia's independence from the Dutch and was granted the highest civilian honor of "Bhoomi Putra" or "Son of the Soil" by the Indonesian government.

will help me there, why not?" But this man, even in the last moment he says, "Nothing doing. I lived my life well. I don't care what happens there. If it is there or not, I don't know. So let me go blind." Hurtling...simply. It is a good way to go.

"So what should I do?" There is a Sanskrit verse, *"Balastavat krida saktaha"* – when you were a child, your playfulness engaged you fully; your playfulness was fulltime. Then you became youthful, all that playfulness looked a little silly. You thought you were getting more serious and purposeful. But then what to do? Your intelligence got hijacked by the hormones. After that you could not see anything.

Suddenly you looked at a man or woman, all kinds of things happened. They were quite okay just last year, but now suddenly... somehow from within, you got poisoned in such a way that everything started to look in a certain way. You will see, once this hormonal hijack is over, you look at a man or a woman, they look just normal. When this was on, when you looked at them, they looked like fire. It consumed you. It was not unreal, it was very real, isn't it?

Then age happened. Old people are simply worried. A child is too engaged in play. You cannot talk to him about the Ultimate. Youth is fully hijacked by hormones. You cannot talk to him about it. Old people are worried about what their hierarchy will be in heaven. You cannot talk to them about it. Then who the hell is there? Someone who is neither a child, nor youthful, nor old, someone who is just life – only to him you can speak.

So don't think of this as your first step or last step. Just be here as a piece of life. That is the best way to be. You are not a young man; you are not an old man. Earth will decide when it should take your body back. When the manure has matured, it will collect it back – the trees are waiting! Don't worry about that. You are just a piece of life. In terms of this life, this is not young, this is not old; this has to mature into something bigger.

And only if you are here as a piece of life, all aspects of life will happen to you. If you sit here as a man, some things will happen to you. If you sit here as a woman, some other things will happen to you. If you sit here as a child, something else will happen to you. If you sit here as a doctor, or an engineer, or an artist, this or that – different things will happen to you. Only if you sit here as a piece of life, everything that can happen to life will happen to you.

Whether you are two days old or you only have two days left, see how to just be here as a piece of life, not identified with any damn thing. Not identified with the earth or the heaven, simply being here. Then, whether we have one day to live or a hundred years to live, what does it matter? When it does not matter, everything that needs to happen to this life will anyway happen to you. And that is willingness. The moment you identify yourself to be a man, you are only willing for certain things. If you say "I am a woman," you are only willing for certain things. If you are here as life, you are willing for everything.

Sadhguru

DEATH IS A FICTION

"Death is a fiction created by people who live their lives in total unawareness. There is only life, life and life alone, moving from one dimension to another, another dimension to another."

The mystery of the "end of life" has consumed man since time immemorial. Though it is considered the universal destination, the word itself evokes fear in many people. From ghost stories and afterlife aspirations, to lectures and philosophies, people have let their imaginations loose on this mysterious event, inventing innumerable ways of coping with the idea.

Articulating the most intricate aspects of death during a sathsang with seekers, Sadhguru pushes aside all misconceptions and throws light on this seemingly dark subject.

Questioner: *We have heard that man should get out of this cycle of birth and death. Can you speak about that?*

Sadhguru: I always insist that you do not believe anything that is not yet your experience. It does not matter who says it. This does not mean disbelieve. You do not know, that is all. Someone tells you a story, you do not know whether it is true or not.

Even if I say something, do not believe this nonsense, but do not disbelieve it either. Just see, "Someone is willing to sit in front of so many people and talk absolute nonsense, something that is totally absurd. Let me see what this is about." If you keep that much openness, the possibility is alive in your life. If you believe it, you will kill it. If you disbelieve it, you will kill it.

About putting an end to the cycle of birth and death, there are many dimensions to the life process. Once the life process passes the dimension of being embodied in a physical frame, we generally consider this as death. When the body becomes unsuitable to sustain life, life has to move on. So it does.

If you have to leave this body, your energies should become feeble. If you have to enter another body, your energies have to become feeble. You can slip out of your body and you can slip into something else if you wish, because your energies have become so feeble that they do not have the vibrancy of normal existence. If the body breaks, your life energies do not become feeble. They are still vibrant, but the body broke for some reason. Now, this being will have a long transition because the vibrancy of the energy is still there, it has to wear itself out.

There is something called as *prarabdha*. Because of this prarabdha, a certain vibrancy is there in life energy. Prarabdha is the allotted karma for one lifetime. If the whole stock that you have comes into one life, you cannot live. You have a warehouse. This warehouse is referred to as *sanchita*. You cannot handle the warehouse of karma, so a retail stock has been given to you to dispense in this life. But generally most people gather more new stock than get rid of the old stock.

This could go on and on and on, not because you are under some punishment or reward. It is just nature finding its own cycle. When a certain awareness arises within you, somewhere you begin to feel the meaninglessness of the cycle. It is all nice, we are enjoying it, but just going on and on does not make sense. When that awareness comes, that is when you start talking about mukti. Mukti means you want to become free from the process of life and death. Not because you are suffering; suffering people cannot attain mukti. You are fine, you are joyful, but you have had enough of kindergarten, you want to move on. However beautiful your school life was, don't you want to go to college? That's all. You have seen enough of it. Now you want to move on.

This being, whatever you call as this "me" right now... let us say you are emptiness, or darkness. I always use negative terminology so that your imagination does not fly away, because if I say "light," then you will start shining all over the place. If I say "God," then you will start doing funny things. This empty darkness that you are – you cannot imagine much about darkness, isn't it? So we always use negative terminology so that your imagination does not fly off and make you very hallucinatory.

This empty space within you is like a bubble. Karma is the wall of the bubble. Without karmic substance you have no existence. Karma is not your enemy; it is only because of karmic substance you are glued to the body. If all your karma is removed, you cannot be held in the body. It is a bubble. Even though you slip out of the physical body, this bubble is on, and once it loses its vibrancy, it will find another body naturally.

When you say "I want mukti," what you are saying is, you want to prick the bubble in such a way that this emptiness, which is enclosed within the bubble, bursts. Let us say we blow bubbles here now. The moment they burst, the air inside the bubble has become a part of everything. Mukti means just that. Enlightenment also means the same thing. If you are not aware of this already, for most beings, their moment of enlightenment and their moment of leaving the body is the same. Just a few who know the tricks of the body, who know the fundamental mechanics of the body, manage to retain the body for a certain period of time.

If the life energies become overly intense, you cannot keep the body. If the life energies become feeble, you cannot keep the body. Only if the energy is in a certain band of intensity you can hold on to the body. If you raise the intensity beyond a certain pitch, you will leave. If you drop it below a certain level, you will leave. These are the two types of yoga that you see in the world. One is withdrawing, withdrawing so that you become more and more feeble so that you can go. Another is revving it up to a high pitch of intensity, so that the physical cannot hold you anymore.

Two types of yogas are being done – some to become feeble, some to become intense. Socially, the intense thing may be more appreciated, but it does not mean anything. What somebody thinks of you has no existential relevance. It has some social relevance, but existentially, what the world thinks about you or above all, what you think about yourself, has no relevance at all. I should tell you a joke. It is getting dead serious, with all this death and beyond!

One day the Pope died. Naturally, being the Pope, he progressed towards heaven. At the gates of heaven, Saint Peter was sitting on a tall security stool smoking a Cuban cigar. Pope went and looked at this ghastly scene of Saint Peter smoking and that too a Cuban cigar – a banned one. Peter blew the smoke in his face and asked, "Okay man, who are you?"

Pope was totally taken aback, *What is this!* Anyway, he held back and said, "I am the Pope."

"What about it, Popie? Move on."

He said, "How dare you! I am God's representative on the planet. My name is Pope."

Peter took another deep lungful of smoke, blew it at his face and said, "Aey Popie, move on. Every day, all kinds of guys come here and want to go in. Move on."

The Pope said, "How dare you say such things to me! If you want, you ask God! I am his representative on the planet."

"Is that so? Let me see." Peter raised his voice and said, "Hey Boss, there is somebody out here who claims to be your representative on the planet. His name is Pope. Do you know him?"

A grave voice from inside the gate said, "I do not know anybody like that."

"The Boss doesn't know you. Move on, man, enough!"

Pope was distraught. *What is this! How can the old man say he doesn't know me! Must be Alzheimer's.* "You ask Jesus. He knows me. I am his representative on the planet."

So Peter once again raised his voice and said, "Hey Sonny, there is somebody out here who claims to be your representative on the planet. His name is Pope. Do you know him?"

A gentle voice from inside said, "I do not know anybody like that."

"Enough man, Sonny doesn't know you. Move on."

By now, Pope was really breaking up and said, "How can this be?! How can they let me down like this? No, you ask the Holy Ghost, he knows me. I am his representative on the planet."

Saint Peter once again raised his voice and said, "Hey Spooky, there is somebody out here who claims to be your representative on the planet. His name is Pope. Do you know him?"

A very mischievous voice from inside said, "Ah, Pope! Is he here? He is the one who spread all those malicious stories about me and Mary. Don't you let him in."

Whatever you think about yourself, whatever the world thinks about you right now does not mean a damn thing existentially. When you say spirituality, you are seeing how to progress existentially – not socially, not psychologically, not emotionally. You want to progress on the existential level. You want to go somewhere on that level, because your emotion, your society, your psychology is all just pure imagination. Maybe sometimes pleasant imagination, but still imagination. The progression of a being beyond his body is not dependent upon who he was in the world, what he thought of himself or what everyone thought of him. It simply depends on how conscious he is, what he has generated beyond the physical within himself.

Why human birth is considered so valuable is mainly because of this. Only in this one birth, being a human being, you can use your discrimination and act consciously. It does not matter what kind of life you have lived until now, this moment you can still act consciously. You have lived a most horrible life, it does not matter, this moment you can still act consciously. That freedom and that discretion is always with you.

If this consciousness arises, or if a certain intensity is picked up, or if the intensity is dropped beyond a certain point, you become unsuitable for living in the body. When that situation arises, there are possibilities for you to break the bubble completely. If you want to break the bubble and still retain the body, then you need engineering. You need to know all the tricks. Or you have to do some conscious karma to retain the body. There are any number of things that people do. I do not wish to speak about myself because so many things are happening with me.

For example, Ramakrishna Paramahamsa, a fantastic human being, a very crystallized consciousness. During his own lifetime, people saw him as Godlike, but Ramakrishna was mad about food. He was insane about food. He would be talking to his disciples and say, "Please wait." He would go to the kitchen and ask his wife, Sarada, "What's cooking today?" He was madly taken by food.

Sarada felt so ashamed of him, "Why are you like this? I am not concerned about food. We see you as Godlike, and you are crazy about food. What is this?"

He would say, "It's okay, but what's cooking?"

One particular day she was so ashamed of him, she became angry and angry words flew out of her. Then Ramakrishna said, "When you bring the *thali*[18] on a

---

18 A meal pre-served with various dishes in a single plate. The thali is especially large in Bengal, Ramakrishna's native place.

certain day, if I show no interest in the food, you must know there are only three more days left." Six years later, she took the food to him, and he turned away. Suddenly she remembered, and she broke down and cried. He said, "There is no point crying now, time is up."

He was using food as a conscious karma to create a desire, a conscious desire every day – at least ten times a day he has to think of food to keep the body going. Otherwise if he just sits in one place, he will leave the body. He has planned out some work for himself, so he wants to hold on to the body for some more time. Like this, different yogis create different methods; some are simple, some are very complex, various kinds of processes. Once the bubble is gone and you are just keeping it consciously there, in many ways you are existentially not on account.

This happened about four years ago, I think. Every year, we have been going to the Himalayas, taking a few people. It is called the Himalayan Sacred Walks. You must see the Himalayas before you are too old and too bald for anything. When you still have legs, you must see the Himalayas. Being born in India, if you do not see the Himalayas... Oh, you really missed something of Himalayan magnitude!

From Bhojwas, we go to Gomukh, and from Gomukh to Tapovan. Everyone cannot climb to Tapovan, because it is a very tricky climb. Just a few people go, and I did not go up either that time. Those few went up there and there was a seeress. She was called Bengali Maa. They said they have come with their Guru. The lady asked, "Who is your Guru?" They pulled out a picture of mine and showed it.

She just looked at the picture and said, "He's not here anymore; he has gone long ago."

They said, "No, no, he has come with us."

She said, "No, no, he cannot be here. He's gone long ago."

Because I am not on account. I am still on the voters list, though! Existentially, I am not on account. That is why I can live any way I want. When you are not accountable, you can live any way you want, isn't it? And when you are not on account, you do not need to seek anyone's permission, you can close your account as you please.

Questioner: Sadhguru, a lot of the spiritual traditions talk about the moment of death as the most significant moment of your life. Is that really true?

Sadhguru: All the moments in your life before that moment are most important. If you do not realize that, it is like trying to catch the final moment of your life. You cannot. Unless you have caught many moments in your life as a deep, penetrating experience for yourself, you just cannot catch the final moment of your life.

This whole idea of death as it has been spread around in the world today... let us look at it this way. Did you ever die? No, you have no experience of death. Did you ever see a dead man? You may have seen dead bodies, but did you ever see a dead man?

Questioner: No.

Sadhguru: Did you ever see somebody who actually died and came back? No. There may be a near-death experience. Near is not good enough. Near water is not as good enough as water. Some people have nearly died, that is not good enough.

You have not experienced it, you have not seen it, nor have you had first-hand information from anyone. From where did you get this idea that there is something called as death? Death is a fiction created by ignorant people. Death is the creation of people who live their lives in total unawareness. There is only life, life and life alone, moving from one dimension to another, another dimension to another.

The process of life you can also refer to as death. You can say "I am living right now" or you can say "I am dying right now." Actually, from the day you are born you are slowly dying. One day the process will be complete. Right now it is on the way. You may be thinking you are going many places, but as far as your body is concerned, without a moment's distraction, it is going straight to the grave, nowhere else.

Is death okay or not okay? Even these kinds of questions which are coming up are silly, because whether you say it is okay or not okay, anyway you will die. Every moment you are playing between life and death – actually it is so. This inhalation, exhalation... You inhaled, life happened. If you exhaled and did not inhale again, death happens, isn't it? In yoga we say inhalation is life, exhalation is death. You exhale, and if you do not take in the next inhalation it dislodges you from the body. So fragile, isn't it? Something so fragile is the basis of your existence here. Death is walking with you every step. It is so close all the time.

There is nothing wrong with death; it has to happen. Only because there is death, there is life. You need to understand that the moment you are born, you have a death sentence upon you. When, where, and how is the only question, but you are on death row. Your death is confirmed. We do not know whether you will get educated or not; we do not know whether you will get married or not; we do not know whether you will know joy or not; we do not know whether you will know misery or not; but we know one day you will die. That one thing is guaranteed.

This whole fear about death has come simply because you have no idea what it is. You have formed ideas about everything. But it does not matter what ideas you have formed about life, when you are confronted with the moment of death, you really do not know anything. That is one space of life which has remained uncorrupted by the human mind. Everything else we have corrupted. Whatever was supposed to be sacred, all these things are hugely corrupted by human minds. Love, relationships, God, Divinity – everything they have corrupted and twisted out whichever way they want. Death is one thing that they are still clueless about – though a lot of people would like to talk authoritatively about it. They know they are going to go to heaven; they are dead sure about it. If they are so sure, I don't see what they are waiting for!

They are doing everything not to go to heaven. Why? If you are so sure you are going to a wonderful place, a better place than this, then you must hurry up. But because you are not sure, you talk. You are not 100% sure where you will go or what will happen to you. Just to solace yourself, just to be able to psychologically handle life, you create all these things. But essentially, the very idea of death has come to you because people have been talking about it without knowing about it. Otherwise, if your societies did not speak about it, you would just know the way you are right now, your present existence, is not permanent. That you would know, but you would not have any other ideas about it. Even now you do not have any idea about it; you imagine that you have.

Your whole life, you are only living in your mind, not in this world. Just look back and see, in the last twenty-four hours, how many moments have you truly experienced the way they are? You are only thinking about life. You are not experiencing life. You are a psychological existence, not an existential existence. Whatever happens in your mind is irrelevant, because you can imagine anything and think it is true. What happens in your mind, what you think and feel has nothing to do with the reality of life, but right now, humanity has invested so much towards what they think and feel. What this essentially means is that your own petty creation that you create in your mind has become so important for you that you are missing the magnificent creation of the Creator. You missed it all.

This body is just a piece of this Earth. It has popped up from this Earth and it will go back to this Earth. Before you and me came here on this planet, a countless number of people walked this planet. Where are they? All topsoil. You will also become topsoil – unless someone buries you real deep, fearing that you may rise from the dead! This body right now is a debt that you have taken from the planet.

Let us say I give you a one-million-dollar loan today – I will not, I am just telling you! And in ten years' time, you made this one million into one hundred million. After ten years, if I come looking for you, what would you do with me? You would welcome me, I am your dear friend, isn't it? You would give back my million and maybe an extra million, and send me. Suppose I gave you one million today and in ten years' time, you squandered it completely and lost everything. If I come looking for you, what would you feel? Terror. When a debtor comes, it is worse than death for most people.

This is just the same. This body is a loan from the planet. If you have done something truly wonderful out of it, when the moment to pay back the loan comes, you would give it back joyfully. Otherwise, when the moment to pay back the loan comes, you will shiver in your pants.

How you die is in many ways indicative of how you have lived within yourself. It is in that context that traditions may have spoken about the significance of the last moment. And the last moment is significant because if you can maintain awareness at that moment, the quality of that moment endures beyond that. You can try this with your sleep. Tonight when you go to sleep, create a very loving atmosphere within yourself. Be very conscious and loving and fall asleep with a big smile on your face. You will see that this quality will perpetuate through the night. When you wake up in the morning, you will see this quality radiating out of you.

Eastern cultures have always insisted that you must sleep in a particular way, you must wake up in a particular way. For all these things, they fixed particular methods as to how to do it. Yoga and spiritual processes have specific ways as to how to go to bed and how to wake up in the morning. When that moment of transition is of a certain quality, naturally that quality endures. When that moment of death is of a certain level of awareness or pleasantness, naturally that pleasantness and awareness will endure. When you are here in this embodied form, you have a discretionary mind. Right now, whatever is offered to you, you can choose. If I give you a mud ball and an apple, you can look at them and eat the apple, not the mud ball. But once you have left your body and your discretionary mind, after that you do not have choices, you only move by tendencies. Every individual acquires a certain tendency depending upon the impressions that he has taken in. Even now, please see, with those who are alive, unless a person exercises a certain level of awareness and intellect, he will function only by his tendencies. Even now, so many people on this planet are causing misery to themselves not because they want to. They are going by their tendencies, they have become compulsive. Compulsiveness simply means that you are not exercising your discriminatory intellect, you are not aware enough to do that. That is absolutely true even now, but once you have dropped the discriminatory intellect completely, you will have no choices. You will go according to your tendencies.

In that final moment, if you create a certain tendency of pleasantness, then the transition of going beyond the body will be very pleasant. Generally, in almost every culture, this awareness is there to some extent. When a person is near death, that is not the time for anger, remorse or hatred. All those things you drop and do the best that you can do to create a pleasant atmosphere around him.

It once happened. There were two sisters, Mithilda and Lucia, who had a feud between them, and they had not spoken to each other for thirty-five years. Mithilda, at the age of eighty-seven, was about to die. She was on her deathbed. Then Lucia came to see her. Mithilda looked at her and said, "Okay, I am going to die. If I die, all that I hold against you is forgiven, but just in case if I make it, it is all the way it was. Everything is just the way it was. You better know that."

You waste life and try to make use of death. You cannot. If you maintain a certain level of awareness right through your life, the moment of passing can also happen in your awareness. You live a life of unawareness and you expect to be aware at that moment – such things don't happen to people.

You just practice this tonight, the last moment of passing from wakefulness to sleep, maintain your awareness. See if you can, but you will see if you try to be aware, you will be awake. Only when you lose your awareness you will fall asleep. Just use this as a method every day. Go at it with total perseverance, and you will see in a few days you will get there, where at the final moment you are aware. Suddenly everything about your life, the fundamental quality of your life will change just by doing this one simple thing. Phenomenal things that you have never imagined possible will become a reality if you can just manage a moment of awareness – that moment when you are transiting from wakefulness to sleep. If you do that, you will also transit from life to death in full awareness.

Questioner: What can I do to make myself aware?

Sadhguru: Awareness is on many different levels. What you are aware of is all that exists for you. This must be understood. Right now where you are sitting – don't turn back and see – there is a huge dinosaur standing behind you, but you are not aware of it. It does not matter that such a huge animal is standing there, you are not aware of it, so it does not exist for you. Only what you are aware of exists for you. Right now, your awareness is limited to a small aspect of your life. The whole aspect of spirituality means to become aware of everything that you are, so that before you go, you know life, you experience life in its totality. To live and to live totally, that is spirituality; so that you know life in all dimensions, you do not go just knowing a little part of your life.

If you want to know all of it, how? If we have to use an analogy, let us say there is a bulb and we turn down its voltage. It lights up only so much, and only that much we see. If you turn up the voltage, suddenly you are able to see much more because the light has spread. Awareness is just like this. Right now, your energies, your body, your emotion, your mind, are functioning with a certain limited voltage. If you crank up the voltage, suddenly you start seeing so many things which were not in your experience until that moment.

In a way, to put it very simply, to put it technically, you need to turn up your voltage. You can turn up your voltage simply with your enthusiasm, but that will not take you all the way. There are other kinds of technologies to turn up your voltage in a certain way where all the time you are high.

Within myself right now, I am absolutely drunk. Not with alcohol, okay? I never touched it. I am totally drunk within myself. I am balanced enough and logical enough to handle any situation. All the time I am fully drunk on one level, on another level I am perfectly sane. If I want to flip, any moment I will flip. If you are like this – inside you are fully charged, outside you are control – this is what is needed in your life if you want to experience life in its totality. You try to exercise control over your life, and you started putting this control over your very process of life, so life is happening like a trickle. Life within you should happen like a huge explosion, but outside it is fully controlled.

You will see initially when you go into a phase like this, even the outside tends to happen like an explosion for some time, but within a limited period of time you will gather some control over it. Outside is controlled, inside is an explosion. That is how it should be. Every moment of your life, within you, life should be an absolute explosion. Outside of you it is properly controlled. When it is like this you will get to use your physical body, your mind, your emotion everything that you have to its fullest extent. Things that you never thought you were capable of, you suddenly start doing simply because your voltage is full.

Questioner: Sadhguru, we have so many choices about life. The more aware I become, the more choices I am seeing. But are there any choices about my death?

Sadhguru: There are, definitely. What you are referring to as death is just the last moment of life – that final moment when you transcend the limitations of your physical body. That happens only once in your lifetime. Almost everything in your life may happen many times over. But this one thing happens only once in your lifetime and it is the last thing that you do. The last thing that you do in your life is death. I want you to understand death as life, not something else. Everything that you can experience is life. Death is the last act of your life. Is it not important that you choose to make it happen gracefully and wonderfully? If you are fearful of it, if you are ignorant of the ways of life and you create resistance towards it, naturally you will miss that possibility.

A yogi always wants to know the time and the date of his death ahead of time. He fixes it. Many years before, he says, "On this day, at this time, I will leave," and he leaves, because he has created the necessary awareness within himself to leave consciously, without damaging the body. Like you take off your clothes and walk away, like that you take off your body and walk away. If you can do that, that is the ultimate possibility in your life. Once you have gained this much awareness to know where you, as a being, and this physical body which you gathered are connected – where the connection is, what is the hold – then you can disentangle yourself whenever the moment is right for you.

Is this suicide? Definitely not. Suicide happens out of frustration, anger, fear, out of the inability to bear with suffering. This is neither suicide nor euthanasia. This is about being so aware that you know when life has completed its cycle and you walk out of it. And this is not death either; this is known as samadhi where a human being has developed sufficient awareness within himself where he can separate who he is from the physicality that he has gathered. In that level of awareness one can leave. If you do not attain such a level of awareness, at least if you manage certain things, you can make that last moment very graceful, pleasant, joyful and blissful for yourself.

What I have seen is, most people die with a sense of being lost, in disappointment or fear. Even those people who seem to die peacefully, they die in disappointment and frustration. Being bewildered that it is getting over, despite all that hope and activity – there is a sense of being deceived by life. That is what you will see at the moment of death. It is my wish and my blessing that this should not happen to you.

When you die, you must die joyously with a huge smile on your face. I have seen many people around me dying joyously with a big smile on their face. That is a wonderful way to go. I want to see that you die that way. And if you want to die joyously, you should know how to live beyond your limitations right now. If you do not learn how to transcend your limitations when you are alive, you dying joyously does not arise at all.

When we say a spiritual process, we are not just helping people to live well. We also help people to die well. Helping people to die well does not mean we will assist them to die, as euthanasia enthusiasts are talking about – not in that sense. It is very important that the moment of passing from the physicality to the beyond, from being embodied to being disembodied, happens in utmost awareness and grace. We can create that moment for every human being, if that human being is willing to cooperate and pay some attention to himself now. If one wants to exercise this choice, a certain amount of preparation is needed. As I said earlier, if you can practice this every day, that you move from your wakefulness to sleep in awareness, if you manage that, this last moment of passing from life to death will happen absolutely gracefully for you.

Questioner: I work in a clinic with lots of cancer patients. Even if it is obvious that they will die, they are full of hope. Doctors make all the efforts, but the truth is they have to die. I cannot understand where this hope is coming from because it is clear that people have to go, they have to die, right?

Sadhguru: Now that you say anyway a person has to die, shall we let him die? Death will anyway happen, you do not have to support it. It is life that needs support. Death does not need your support. It will happen. Life needs your support because life is a brief happening, death is a very big one. About life and death, if we use the analogy of light and darkness, you would understand this better.

Light has always been glorified. You say Divine light. You will not say Divine darkness. But you tell me, which is more all-encompassing? Light is a brief happening, it needs a source which burns. And whatever kind of light source, whether it is a light bulb, or the major source of light for you right now, the sun, both will burn out one day. We know that today. When there is no light, darkness is all-pervading. It is in the lap of darkness that light happens here and there. So, which should you refer to as Divine?

Darkness has always been associated with evil in the West. But in India, when an ignorant person comes, we refer to Divine as light. When an evolved person comes, we refer to Divine as darkness. Because when a person is ignorant, if you say, "Divine is darkness," he does not want to go there, because darkness is something that he has always feared. Death is something he always feared. Dark corners in the street are always something that he feared. But when a person has evolved beyond certain limitations, if he has tasted something beyond the physical, then we always refer to the Divine as darkness. Shiva is known as the Dark One.

Your idea of life is just keeping the physical body alive. The physical body is something that you have borrowed from this Earth and you have to shed it. There is no question about it. It does not charge you any interest, but it takes back every atom that it gave you. Nobody can carry a single atom from here. It is just a question of physical body – but it needs support.

Every day you are eating whatever you can afford to eat. This is a life-support system. For someone else, food is not going in because there is cancer in the throat. They are trying to put it into the stomach directly. Whatever they know they are doing. It is okay, but at some point, there is no meaning just going on stretching it. There is no meaning to stretch life by making the physical body exist for a few more days at enormous pain for the person.

The culture should also learn to let people die peacefully; it is very important. Because existing for another one month or two or three months will not make any difference for anyone. But because the only thing that people know is physical body, they do not want to let it go.

People on the spiritual path shed their body consciously when the body is in full health. A good body, a body which is in utmost wellness – they leave it because they have known something other than the physical. For them, dropping the physical is not a big issue. When people have not known anything other than the physical, physical is the biggest issue. That is why they are stretching it. Divine should enter, it is time.

Questioner: Namaste Sadhguru. A month ago my mother passed away. In our community, the rituals[19] for the dead are very long and are sometimes very painful for the close ones. I did all those things, but am not really convinced with what I have done. When I asked, "Why am I asked to do all this?" I was not given any explanation. Is there really any meaning to these rituals?

Sadhguru: Whoever conducted all this, did you pay them or did you run away from there?

---

19 Referring to a complex set of rituals performed for the deceased, generally within two weeks of passing away, for which the family is required to provide various items.

Questioner: Whatever they demanded I paid them.

Sadhguru: You paid them, then the job is done. There is no problem. For you, your mother died, it is a big thing; but you need to understand someone else's mother is not dead; they have to live. Their mother, their wife, their children, they all have to live.

You feel that someone is making a business out of your mother's death and you feel angry and frustrated about it. But this is a perpetual business – whatever economic meltdown may happen, people will continue to die. When such an opportunity is there how to let it go? It is a perpetual business.

We complicated these things in so many ways. At the same time, it is not that there is no basis at all to these rituals. No, there is a basis. Unfortunately, over a period of time people distort it and exaggerate things in such a way that it just becomes commerce.

Many people did not treat their mothers well when they were alive. At least for those twelve or thirteen days, they want to do something to feel psychologically free from that. And compared to the fees that the psychiatrists charge these days, this is not much. They are still only asking for cupfuls of rice, grams, nuts and this and that. Maybe they ask you for a cow or footwear, or umbrella – whatever.

Your dead mother definitely cannot use the umbrella, nor does she need the umbrella. If you did not have a body, we would have the sathsang outside in the rain now, isn't it?

Only because you have a body, it gets soaked, it gets sick, all these problems arise. Only because you have a body, you need a roof. Where there is no roof, you need an umbrella. Footwear also, the same thing. Head or foot, same problems, but there is someone else living here who needs all these things.

Not everyone lives the same way, not everyone dies the same way. When I say not everyone lives the same way, all of you being here together for the last three days, all of you are getting up at the same time, eating the same food, going through the same sathsang, but all of you are still not living in the same way, even in these three days. Each individual person is living his own way. So you will all not die the same way.

Right now, if a piece of sky falls upon us and all of us get crushed and die, we still will not die the same way. We may die in the same situation, of the same cause, but we still will not die the same way. Different people die different ways, and when people die in certain ways, a little bit of assistance would do very good things for them, if there was someone aware enough and capable enough to do something about that. A long time ago, there were some people who could do a genuine job on these things. We will set up these death services for people where things will be done properly, not just as a ritual, not as a commercial process but genuinely, what needs to be done.

This man who came for the rituals, did you actually give the cow, or just the money?

Questioner: Money.

Sadhguru: That is okay. Simply bringing the cow, taking it back, selling it again is too much unnecessary transaction. This is okay. This is alright. I am not against commerce. It is just that we must be straight enough to say, "This is commerce." Spiritual process should be handled as spiritual process, and commerce should be handled as commerce, but most of the time, people are mixing up the two. They are trying to handle business like a spiritual process, and spiritual process, generally, like a business. This is going on everywhere.

It happened once that an airplane took off from Austin, Texas. Within a few minutes, after it took off, when it was sufficiently away from the airport, suddenly they found that the engines were failing. The pilot announced to the passengers, "I really don't know what to do. I don't have enough time or altitude to turn around and get back. We just don't know what to do. If someone knows something religious to do, please do it." One man immediately got up, took off his hat and went about collecting money, because generally that is the most religious thing.

About this man who came and collected money for the cow, which is supposed to be exported for your mother's use up there – is there really anything to it? Somewhere way back, I do not know how many generations ago, his great, great, super-great grandfather knew what to do about your mother, but most of them today did not learn anything over generations. Now they are just doing business. Those people knew what to do.

One thing that you need to understand is, when somebody dies – as you know death today – it does not matter whether he happens to be your father, your mother, your husband, your wife, your child, how dear a friend he was – it does not matter. The moment he leaves the body, he has got nothing to do with you, because everything that he knew about you is physical. All that you know about that person and all that they know about you is either the physical body, or mind, or emotion. All these things belong to the sphere of the physical. When he leaves the physical, all those things are gone and there is nothing like "me and my dead father." Once he is dead, he is not your father. He is over.

When you say someone is no more, you are only saying they are no more with us. You are not saying they are really no more. They are just no more with you, the way you knew them. When one leaves the body, for whatever reason, the fundamental reason is because the physical body has become unsuitable to sustain and nourish life. When this happens, what will happen to that being? The physical body and the conscious mind go – the discretionary aspect of his mind, the discretionary choices are gone, but the content of his mind is not gone. He still has the qualities, but he has no discrimination. Once the discretionary mind is gone, he will only proceed according to his tendencies.

Essentially, why death is happening is because these life energies are programmed in a certain way. As we looked at before, if life has to be embodied, it must be in a certain level or range of intensity. If it becomes too intense and goes above a certain point, it will leave the body. Or if it becomes feeble beyond a certain point then it will slip out. This is called as dying naturally, out of old age. People just lie down, close their eyes, and they are gone. Nothing broke – his liver did not go wrong, his kidneys or his heart did not go wrong – life simply became feeble and slipped out. That means he lived his full term. Whatever this particular life was programmed for, it went through its full course, so it leaves.

Only very few, rare human beings leave because of excessive intensity; a certain number leave because of old age; most of the others die because something broke. Either you crashed your car or you smoked yourself, drank yourself or worked yourself to death, or something else broke – in some way, you made the physical body inhospitable for life. Something went wrong in this mechanism; now it cannot host a life, so life leaves. But it is still in a certain level of intensity that it could have continued to be embodied for a much longer period.

When life leaves like this, then it cannot find another body immediately; it has to hang. Let us say, by normal course, he would have died after ten years, but today, because of excessive work or stress or whatever, his heart broke and he died today. Ten more years were there for him approximately, but he left the body. Because he has left the body, because he has lost the discretionary mind, because he has lost the ability to perform any kind of karma as such, these ten years may become a hundred years without the body. With the body, with the discretionary mind, this would have been over in ten years, but without them, this may take a hundred years or five hundred years; we do not know.

This depends on various things, depending upon what kind of karmic substance he carries. Knowing these things, we created a whole science as to how to help people beyond their body – because most people die of infections and diseases and ailments. We could not help them when they were in the body maybe because we could not figure out what the ailment was, or he did not get the treatment, or something happened, and he died. Now we want to help him in such a way that he dissolves this quickly, so that he does not hang around for too long. There is a whole science behind these rituals.

This man to whom you gave the cow money, you are giving it to him because his great, great, super-great grandfather knew what to do. You are still paying him for the knowledge that the super-great grandfather knew. This fool also should have learned, but somewhere it all got dislocated. Now it has just become a plain ritual where he has learned a few mantras and you don't know what it is to check. He could be abusing you in Sanskrit. As you were feeling he was terrible, he must have looked at you and started abusing you in Sanskrit language! You don't know. Probably while you were cursing him, he was cursing you and your mother. Cow business is happening, but nothing else is happening.

These things have unfortunately happened because modern societies have become more and more superficial by the day, for which we will pay a price. Here and hereafter, in both we will pay a very big price because we are becoming extremely superficial with the life process.

Suppose you die, and someone sends a picture of you, we could do something. Sometimes we can do a lot, sometimes we can do little, sometimes we can do an absolute job, depending upon who it is. And we won't tell you what we have done, but we will do something for sure. For some, we can do a great amount of help; for some, we can just push them a little bit. Depending upon how they died, why they died, who they are – various aspects are involved in this.

This is a very essential science, a very essential understanding of life, because everyone dies, everyone loses somebody who is dear to them. At some point in our life, we will lose someone who is dear to us. Definitely, we would like to see that something nice happens to them. We had means for all these things but now, we got English educated, and we are ashamed of these things – because now your mother's death is a mumbo jumbo. No, this is not mumbo jumbo.

All these things should not be business. There are a few things which should never be commercialized: education, health, and spiritual process. Once these three are commercialized, that society is heading down. It may take some time but it will head down. You can see this happening with the most affluent countries. Wherever they made education, health and religion a great commercial activity, they are heading down. It is bound to happen in any society.

We are picking that up in India in a big way now. We will see, because of this economic boom, this cow-business will happen a lot for some time. And then we will head down. There is no other way.

A few things should be kept off commerce, it is extremely important. That is why we are looking for volunteers all the time, so that dedicated people conduct certain things, not people who are looking for livelihood.

Questioner: What do the death rituals do for a person?

Sadhguru: When a person dies, the life energy does not leave the body all at once. For all practical purposes one may be dead, but still – if you are a doctor, or if you are old enough to have seen enough deaths around you, or if you happen to be running an undertaker's business, you would know this – when a person dies, the hair and the nails on a dead body continue to grow up to 11-14 days, sometimes up to 40 days. Are you aware of this? You will need a shave even then.

The hair growing means the stubble will come out. If a man had a clean shave and died today, you will see if you keep his body in a morgue for three days, after three days he will have stubble. Hair is continuing to grow. Nails will continue to grow. That means life is active in some form.

Maybe not enough to recognize him as a live person, but life is on in a minimal form, because the receding of life from the physical body happens slowly.

There are five dimensions of vital energies, or *pranas,* in the physical system. These five can be further classified as per specific functions. They are known as: Samana, Prana, Udana, Apana and Vyana. The first thing that leaves the system at the time of death is Samana, or the body's "fire." When Samana starts receding, the body starts to become cold. The next to recede is Prana, the "air." When that is gone, the breath and thought stops. Once Samana and Prana have left, for all practical purposes, one is dead; medically you will be declared dead, once these two things leave. The others are still there and will recede slowly.

Udana starts receding between 6 to 12 hours' time. Udana represents sound or vibration. As it recedes, there will be certain withdrawal sounds in the body. Maybe medically, they have found ways to listen to the body's sounds and reverberations, while Udana is receding. Once Udana has gone, the possibility of life coming back into that body has been sealed off. Once the sounds or reverberations of life are gone, then it is 99.999% certain that life will not return to this body.

Apana, the body's "water," starts receding between 6 to 18 hours' time. Vyana, the "earth," which is in charge of the preservative nature of the body, starts receding between 12 to 18 hours. Once Vyana begins to recede, rigor mortis will set in. As long as that is there, the body is still flexible and feels like it is alive, but it is dead because the Samana and Prana have already left. Of the five, the Vyana recedes slowest, so the bondage with the earth breaks last.

A yogi with sufficient mastery would be able to gather all the five at once and leave. Or if for some reason, he chooses to leave Vyana behind, he can also do that. Otherwise, Vyana takes somewhere between 11 to 14 days to recede. That is why all the death rituals are within that time. In this tradition, they say the body must be burnt one-and-a-half hours after death happens, to make sure everything leaves fast, and the being does not linger on. The rituals after the cremation are done with *asthi*, or the ash, that stays alive for quite some time.

If a yogi has done enough work upon these five, when he leaves he will gather everything. He does not want to linger with a dead creature. When he vacates, he vacates totally. He does not want to leave anything of himself behind – which is a good way to leave. To leave like this, one needs certain mastery over his own energies. If such a mastery is not there, if you do not know how to do it, someone who knows how to do it will do it to you after you are dead.

Suppose you are living in a rented house and your landlord asks you to vacate and you vacate in parts – you take your furniture, but you leave your kitchen things; you take your kitchen things, but you leave your bed things; because you want to keep coming back and do something with the house. If the landlord sees that you are hesitating to vacate and are vacating in parts, then he will take everything and throw it out.

That is exactly what needs to be done. That is why the ritual, if it is done properly. But unfortunately as I said earlier, these rituals have just become a kind of ritualistic circus without the necessary science behind them, without the necessary understanding and expertise – mostly, not always. There are still people who can do it well.

If you do not know how to vacate, if you are too attached to the dwelling in which you have been and you want to vacate in installments, someone else can push you out a little bit. That can always be done, because so many people, almost everybody on the planet is beginning to die unawares without the necessary understanding of the life mechanism within themselves.

So we have set up this death service for people not just as a ritual, not as a commercial process but genuinely, where things will be done properly. The main problem with ritual is when the level of integrity drops in the social fabric, all rituals will turn corrupt. These rituals were created when the sense of integrity and commitment for each other was so strong that there was no room for any kind of misuse. That is when these rituals were created, knowing that one human being will never misuse the other human being's wellbeing in any sense. But when the general fabric of integrity has gone down in the social structure, then all rituals will be under suspicion because there is room for misuse.

If I teach someone how to handle the dead, they want to

display it to their friends – how they can make the dead dance or do something. This kind of ridiculous sense of childishness has entered humanity, and being whimsical is considered as freedom, which is a very dangerous way to go. Once people consider going by their whims as freedom, then nothing of any profoundness can be brought about in the society. All you can do is eat, drink, dance and fall down at the end of the party. When you get fed up with the party, have an overdose and die, we need to set up services for them also.

We are developing a few people who can handle the dead because a large segment of humanity is growing up, living, and will die without any understanding of the life mechanism, as to how it happens within themselves. Are there any volunteers for handling the dead? What is needed is just a certain level of integrity and a certain dedication to do certain type of sadhana which is different from normal sadhana, which can easily be set up here. And it is a very important service that is needed in the world. It is not about just conducting some ritual and pleasing people and doing something pleasant or unpleasant and going away. It is about doing something that works for the dead: the service is for the dead, not for the living. It is an express need that can be delayed because the dying do not wait.

Every day people are dying, nothing is being done for them. And they did not live with the awareness that they can do it for themselves. If people lived with the necessary awareness and the necessary sadhana, then you do not need any ritual; they will handle it themselves. But when they do not have that, it is a very important part of life that death is handled properly.

Questioner: How can we make sure that someone's death is handled properly, even if they did not live with awareness?

Sadhguru: Life is one kind of sound. Death is another kind of sound. Those who cannot hear the sound of death think death is silence. Death is not silence, it is just another kind of sound, but maybe not within the hearing range of a normal ear. Every sound has a form attached to it. The sounds of life have forms of life. The sounds of death have forms of their own. Dealing with these forms is an important part of making life a fulfilling process because one who does not know how to conduct his death will definitely have problems conducting his life. People have gotten used to living a botched-up life – to be anxious, insecure, hateful, jealous, and in various states of unpleasantness through the day – slowly humanity has begun to see it as normal.

None of these things are normal. These are abnormalities. Once you accept them as part of life they become normal because the majority has joined the gang of unpleasantness. They are all saying, "Unpleasantness is normal. Being nasty to each other is normal. Being nasty to myself is normal."

Someone trusted that you would be doing good things at least to yourself and said, "Do unto others what you do unto yourself." I am telling you, never do unto others what you are doing to yourself! By being with people, I know what they are doing to themselves is the worst thing. Fortunately, they are not doing such horrible things to others. Only once in a way they are giving a dose to others, but to themselves they are giving it throughout the day. If you are a very blissful human being, what he is saying is great. When you are practicing to go to hell – self-torture so that the devils cannot succeed, it is a botched-up life.

On a certain day, a man who had ambitions for his business, decided to shift his business from a smaller location to a better location in the town so that he will have a more vibrant business going in the future. Then his wife sent him a floral bouquet, and when the bouquet came, he opened it and he saw the note. The note said, "Rest in peace."

He got really mad; he knew his wife could not have done this. So he called the florist and said, "You fool! I have moved into a new premises. I am looking for vibrant business, and you send a card wishing me to rest in peace."

Then the florist said, "Oh that's nothing! You don't even have to get angry for this."

He said, "What do you mean?"

"Can you imagine, somewhere a funeral is happening, and there the note reads, 'Congratulations on your new location.' You cannot even get angry with me!"

So instead of just wishing them, we thought we will do something for both "Rest in peace" and for "Congratulations on your new location." If the new location is a better place, definitely we must congratulate them. And the way the majority of the people are living right now within themselves, any damn place will be better than that. If you send them to hell, they may think it is heaven. It is a relative experience.

We have started a certain process called Kala Bhairava Karma. Not just to wish them, but to ensure that their new location is in a good place. How can we ensure this? Let us say someone died somewhere. When someone dies, you think he is dead, but as far as that person is concerned, he just lost his body and everything that he knew as life. When he lost his body, he also lost his discretionary mind.

For example, when people drink alcohol or take drugs, all that is happening to them is they lose their discrimination. If they do it in a place that is happy, where they are all laughing, when they lose their discretion, they become happier and happier. But the same people, if they are in an unpleasant condition and they drink or drug, they become more and more unpleasant. Have you seen this? The drink or the drug by itself is not causing pleasantness or unpleasantness; it is pulling down the discretionary mind. Once the discretionary mind is pulled down, if you create a little pleasantness, pleasantness will multiply. If you create a little unpleasantness, unpleasantness will multiply. There are some people, when they drink they become very pleasant; there are some other people, when they drink they become hugely unpleasant. Whatever is their condition, it gets exaggerated because the discretionary mind has come down.

This is exactly what happens when someone loses one's body – but on a much more absolute scale. There is no discretionary mind at all. Even in a drunkard it is there, even in a child it is there, but in the dead it is completely absent. Whatever his tendencies, may be, they will multiply. If he avalanches into a hugely unpleasant state, we call this hell. If he rolls up into a very pleasant state, we call this heaven. Hell and heaven are not geographically located places. It is individual human beings. Because of loss of discretion, they roll up into something big, one way or the other.

In this culture, if somebody is dying, they have taught you some mantra. The idea is, you utter this or that mantra to create a certain pleasantness, to make sounds which will bring a certain vibrance into the dead which will be of pleasantness. So, certain mantras were created because the people who engineered this culture were not ruled by emotion or thought; they were just ruled by their awareness and perception. If someone is dying, you sit here and chant. Not hold their hand and do this and that – just sit and chant.

Traditionally, in India people always chose not to die with their loved ones, because if you die among your family, so many emotions will come. This may be completely unthinkable in the West, because they want to die in the comfort of their family, but that is not a wise thing. It is truly wise for a person to choose a space which is spiritually conducive, which is vibrant in a certain way, and there he leaves with as much grace as possible. If you have lived your life with grace, it becomes extremely important that you die with grace.

If people want to die, when old age comes, they will move to Kashi[20] to die alone, not to die among the family, because if you die among the family you will look at them with attachment. You are not able to part; unpleasantness will come and that unpleasantness will snowball into something terrible for you – and it is also not good for others. When death comes, you move away and die alone. These things are not done out of emotion or out of thought but because of a certain perception and knowledge about the death.

If a person dies of old age, we clearly have 11 to 14 days of time where we can still touch that life in such a way that pleasantness will seep into it. Even if you put a drop of pleasantness into him, this is going to become an ocean of pleasantness after some time, because he has no discretion, he cannot stop it. You start laughing, sometimes you cannot stop laughing, then your discretionary mind kicks in and says, "Enough," and you stop it and go about your work. But if the dead start laughing, they cannot stop; there

---

20 Also known as Varanasi, is over 3500 years old, making it one of the oldest cities in the world. In India, Hindus consider it to be the holiest of holy cities.

is no discretionary mind to kick in and do something. It will just snowball into an extreme sense of pleasantness, which is generally referred to as heaven.

In case someone died below 40 years of age – who was a very young vibrant life, where life is still vibrant, but the body broke and became inhospitable for the life process – then up to 48 days after death very easily we can put a drop of pleasantness into that being. If it is very vibrant, we can influence that life up to 90 days. If he is 50–55 years of age, but he is an active, vibrant life and he died because he broke his body for some reason, then we can influence him up to 48 days.

This has been very much a part of yogic culture that if someone dies and does not have the awareness to conduct his death properly, then someone else does it for him. But unfortunately, probably in the last 100-150 years, these traditions have become largely dormant and what is left is all corrupt and has become purely commercial. This has been bothering me for a while. So, we are starting these processes right here in the ashram. Using the Linga Bhairavi as the energy base, we will conduct certain processes for the dead. If someone that you know dies or someone else that your friend knows, within 14 days if they send us a piece of their clothing, a certain process will happen.

We would like people to live their lives blissfully. If they do not live blissfully, at least they must die peacefully. If they don't even do that, we want to do something after they die. So even if you are dead we won't let you go. How is that?

Sadhguru

APPENDIX 1

ISHA YOGA PROGRAMS

Isha Yoga distills powerful, ancient yogic methods for a modern person, creating peak physical, mental, and emotional wellbeing. This basis of total wellbeing accelerates inner growth, allowing each individual to tap the wealth of vibrant life within oneself. Sadhguru's introductory program, Inner Engineering, introduces Shambhavi Mahamudra – a simple but powerful kriya (inner energy process) for deep inner transformation.

The uniqueness of Isha Yoga is that it is offered as a 100% science. It draws on the ancient yogic principle that the body is the temple of the spirit and that good health is fundamental to personal and spiritual development. Scientifically structured, it promotes beneficial changes in one's inner chemistry to accelerate the release of physical, mental and emotional blocks and produce a life-transforming impact of profound experience, clarity and boundless energy.

The programs are designed for a balanced development of an individual, to bring a spiritual dimension into one's perception without disturbing the process of one's life. Thus, ordinary people have the possibility to have powerful spiritual experiences while balancing normal family and social situations.

www.ishayoga.org

INTRODUCTORY PROGRAMS

Inner Engineering

Inner Engineering is an intensive seven-day program, the foundation for exploring higher dimensions of life is established by offering tools that enable one to re-engineer one's self through the inner science of yoga. Once given the tools to rejuvenate themselves, people can optimize all aspects of health, inner growth, and success. For those seeking professional and personal excellence, this program offers keys for meaningful and fulfilling relationships at work, home, community, and most importantly, within one's self. The program also offers the tools necessary to create the balance between the challenges of a hectic career and the inner longing for peace and wellbeing.

The approach is a modern antidote to stress and presents processes from yogic science to purify the system and increase health and inner wellbeing. Program components include transmission of the sacred Shambhavi Mahamudra as well as guided meditations. When practiced on a regular basis, these tools have the potential to enhance one's experience of life on many levels.

Inner Engineering is also available online as a practical approach for inner transformation in a fast-paced world. Designed by Sadhguru, the online course presents tools for an individual to experience life on a deeper level with more awareness, energy and productivity. Inner Engineering Online is an ideal opportunity for those with time and travel constraints to experience the same profound effects of Isha programs, which have benefited millions of people over the past three decades.

www.innerengineering.com

Isha Kriya

Isha Kriya™ is a simple yet potent practice rooted in the timeless wisdom of the yogic sciences. "Isha" refers to that which is the source of creation; "kriya" literally means "internal action." The purpose of Isha Kriya is to help an individual get in touch with the source of his existence, to create life according to his own wish and vision.

Through Isha Kriya, a 12-minute practice, an individual

can pursue immediate and ultimate wellbeing, experiencing success in the social sphere, while nourishing the inner longing for the deeper dimensions of life. Isha Kriya empowers an individual towards a stress-free way of being, and promotes enhanced clarity, heightened energy levels, and a state of peacefulness and joy. Daily practice of Isha Kriya brings health, dynamism and happiness. It has the potential to transform the life of anyone who is willing to invest just a few minutes a day.

Isha Kriya requires no special physical agility or previous experience of yoga to practice. It integrates seamlessly into one's daily life, bringing the possibilities of a spiritual process – which were once available only to yogis and ascetics – to every human being in the comfort of their own home.

www.ishakriya.com

Hata Yoga

Hata Yoga, a two- to three-day residential program at Isha Yoga, is an opportunity to learn Suryanamaskar (sun salutation) along with a series of *asanas* (yoga postures). The program does not require any previous experience in yoga or particular physical agility. Participants need not have gone through any previous Isha Yoga programs. In this one-time program, the postures are imparted in such depth and precision that the one who goes through the program is enabled to practice them at home. Isha Hata Yoga is far beyond being a mere physical exercise, simply bending the body. This comprehensive set of asanas is scientifically designed in such a way that through regular practice, one can attain to a certain mastery over the body and the mind. Isha Hata Yoga not only improves health and wellbeing, it also brings the necessary balance within oneself to experience higher levels of energy.

The Isha Hata Yoga Teacher Training Program offers classical Hata Yoga in its full depth and dimension. Devised by Sadhguru, a realized master, yogi and a profound mystic, this 21-week program is an unparalleled opportunity to be trained in Hata Yoga, derived from a yogic tradition which has been maintained in its full sanctity and vibrancy for thousands of years.

ishahatayoga.com

Isha Yoga for Children

Isha Yoga for Children offers a unique possibility for every child to experience a joyful blossoming of their natural potential. Isha Yoga celebrates the natural gifts within every child, including their sense of wonder and oneness with life. The program introduces children to yoga through playful and joyful exploration, allowing each child to develop and live in optimal health and inner peace.

Isha Yoga for Children consists of an introduction to simple yoga practices, including Shakti Chalana kriya and asanas, as well as the cultivation of a deep sense of responsibility and reverence for life. The program content is presented through fun games and play so that children experience a sense of belonging and unity with life.

Participants of Isha Yoga for Children often experience enhanced concentration and memory, more focus, and improved mind-body coordination. The practices learned are an effective preventative for obesity, asthma, sinusitis, and other chronic ailments.

Sadhguru

APPENDIX 2

ISHA FOUNDATION

Isha Foundation, founded by Sadhguru is an entirely volunteer-run, international, non-profit movement dedicated to cultivating human potential. The Foundation is a human service organization that recognizes the possibility of each person to empower another – restoring global community through inspiration and individual transformation.

With over 150 centers worldwide, this non-religious, not-for-profit, public service movement has over two million volunteers worldwide. It addresses all aspects of human wellbeing. From its powerful yoga programs for inner transformation to its inspiring projects for society and environment, Isha activities are designed to create an inclusive culture that is the basis for global harmony and progress. This approach has gained worldwide recognition and reflects in Isha Foundation's special consultative status with the Economic and Social Council (ECOSOC) of the United Nations.

The Foundation is headquartered at Isha Yoga Center, set in the lush rainforest at the base of the Velliangiri Mountains in southern India, and at the Isha Institute of Inner Sciences on the spectacular Cumberland Plateau in central Tennessee, USA.

www.ishafoundation.org

ISHA YOGA CENTER

Isha Yoga Center, founded under the aegis of Isha Foundation, is located on 150 acres of lush land at the foothills of the Velliangiri Mountains that are part of the Nilgiris Biosphere, a reserve forest with abundant wildlife.

Created as a powerful *sthana* (a center for inner growth), this popular destination attracts people from all parts of the world. It is unique in its offering of all aspects of yoga – *gnana* (knowledge), *karma* (action), *kriya* (energy), and *bhakti* (devotion) and revives the *Guru-shishya paramparya* (the traditional method of knowledge transfer from Master to disciple).

Located at the Center are the Dhyanalinga, Theerthakund, Isha Rejuvenation Center, Isha Home School and Nalanda (a corporate conference center). The center also houses architecturally distinctive meditation halls and program facilities. Spanda Hall (64,000 sq.ft.) is the venue for advanced Isha programs, while the Adiyogi Alayam, a unique 82,000 sq. ft. column-less hall, is an integral part of Sadhguru's vision to offer at least one-drop of spirituality to every individual.

Isha Yoga Center provides a supportive environment for people to shift to healthier lifestyles, improve their relationships, seek a higher level of self-fulfillment, and realize their full potential.

DHYANALINGA

The main feature of the Isha Yoga Center, the Dhyanalinga, is a powerful and unique energy form created by Sadhguru from the essence of yogic sciences. Dhyanalinga is the first of its kind to be completed in over 2000 years. Dhyanalinga is a meditative space that does not ascribe to any particular faith or belief system nor does it require any ritual, prayer, or worship.

The Dhyanalinga was consecrated by Sadhguru after three years of an intense process of *prana pratishtha*. Housed within an architecturally striking pillar-less dome structure, the Dhyanalinga's energies allow even those unaware of meditation to experience a deep state of meditativeness, revealing the essential nature of life. The Dhyanalinga draws many thousands of people every week, who converge to experience a deep sense of inner peace.

A special feature of the complex are the Theerthakunds, consecrated water bodies, energized by rasalingas. There are two Theerthakunds: the Suryakund for men and Chandrakund for women. A dip in these vibrant pools significantly enhances one's spiritual receptivity and is a good preparation to receive the Grace of the Dhyanalinga. The waters of the Theerthakunds also rejuvenate the body, and bring health and wellbeing.

LINGA BHAIRAVI

Adjacent to the Dhyanalinga, near the Isha Yoga Center, is Linga Bhairavi. Linga Bhairavi is an exuberant expression of the Divine Feminine – fierce and compassionate at once. Representing the creative and nurturing aspects of the universe, the Devi allows devotees to go through life effortlessly; all physical aspects of their lives – health, success, and prosperity – will find nourishment. A variety of rituals and offerings are available for one to connect with the Devi's outpouring Grace.

ISHA OUTREACH

Action for Rural Rejuvenation

A long time vision of Sadhguru, Action for Rural Rejuvenation (ARR) is a pioneering social outreach program. This project is a unique, well-defined plan to rejuvenate rural India, the core of India's life-force, to re-vitalize the human spirit and restore the fundamental kinship nature of village society. It aims to create a synthesis of modern and indigenous models of health and prevention through community participatory governance, while offering primary health care services and other services. So far, ARR has helped more than 3 million people in over 4,600 villages, in the southern states of India.

Isha Vidhya

Isha Vidhya, an Isha Education Initiative, is committed to raising the level of education and literacy in rural India and to help disadvantaged children realize their full potentials. The project seeks to ensure quality education for children in rural areas in order to create equal opportunities for all to participate in and benefit from India's economic growth.

With English computer-based education complemented by innovative methods for overall development and blossoming of each individual, Isha Vidhya schools empower rural children to meet future challenges. Sadhguru's intention and goal is to start 206 English "computer friendly" matriculation schools within the next five to seven years, at least one in each taluk in Tamil Nadu. Currently seven schools have been established, benefiting over 3000 students.

Isha Vidhya schools leverage their experience, the tools developed and facilities created to intervene in Government schools. These interventions aim to enhance the quality of education in Government schools and result in several thousands of children benefiting from a meaningful education. Thirty one schools in Coimbatore, Dharmapuri and Salem Districts have been adopted till date.

Project GreenHands

An inspiring ecological initiative of Isha Foundation, Project GreenHands (PGH) seeks to prevent and reverse environmental degradation and enable sustainable living. Drawing extensively on people's participation, the project aims to plant 114 million trees and thus create 14 percent additional green cover in the state of Tamil Nadu.

As a first step, a mass tree planting marathon was held on October 17, 2006. It resulted in 852,587 saplings being planted across 27 districts by more than 256,289 volunteers, setting a Guinness World Record. To date, PGH has planted over 14 million trees.

www.ishaoutreach.org

ISHA REJUVENATION

Surrounded by thick forests at the tranquil foothills of the Velliangiri Mountains, Isha Rejuvenation helps individuals to experience inner peace and the joy of a healthy body. It offers a unique and powerful combination of programs, scientifically designed by Sadhguru, to bring vibrancy and proper balance to one's life energies. The programs contain a synthesis of allopathic, ayurvedic, and siddha treatments, and complementary therapies, along with the sublime wisdom of various ancient Indian sciences and spirituality. These treatments have had a phenomenal impact on the aging process and have led to miraculous recoveries from seemingly hopeless health situations.

All the proceeds of Isha Rejuvenation contribute toward

providing free health care to rural villagers under the Action for Rural Rejuvenation initiative.

ISHA HOME SCHOOL

Isha Home School aims at providing quality education in a challenging and stimulating home-like environment. It is designed specifically for the inner blossoming and the well-rounded development of children.

With its prominent international faculty and Sadhguru's personal involvement in the curriculum, Isha Home School kindles the innate urge within children to learn and know. Focus is given to inculcating life values and living skills while maintaining the rigor of academic excellence as per national and international standards. It does not propagate any particular religion, philosophy, or ideology; rather, it encourages children to seek a deeper experience and inner understanding of the fundamentals of life.

ISHA SAMSKRITI

Located at the Isha Yoga Center, Isha Samskriti is an education system that provides an ideal environment for children to unfold in harmony within themselves and with the world around them. As in the ancient Gurukuls of India, where students lived and learned in proximity of their Guru, the Isha Samskriti children grow up as an integrated part of the Isha Yoga Center amongst the brahmacharis and residents – all under the guidance of Sadhguru.

In an atmosphere of dedication, discipline and focus, each

aspect of the child's lifestyle is carefully chosen to orient them towards their inner nature. A unique blend of yogic practices, Indian classical arts such as Bharatanatyam and Carnatic Music, and martial arts such as Kalaripayattu, bring balance and stability to the child's body and mind. The children develop into dynamic, capable and dedicated human beings whose presence will be a blessing to the world.

ISHA BUSINESS

Isha Business is a venture that aims to bring a touch of Isha into the homes and environments of the community and to ultimately enrich people's lives. This opportunity is made available through numerous products and services, from architectural designs, construction, interior design, furniture design and manufacturing, landscape design, handicrafts and soft furnishings, to designer outfits from Isha Raiment. All profits from this venture are used to serve the rural people of India through Isha Foundation's Action for Rural Rejuvenation initiative.

HOW TO GET TO ISHA YOGA CENTER

Isha Yoga Center is located 30 km west of Coimbatore, a major industrial city in South India, that is well connected by air, rail and road. All major national airlines operate regular flights into Coimbatore from Chennai, Delhi, Mumbai, and Bangalore. Train services are available from all the major cities in India. Regular bus and taxi services are also available from Coimbatore to Isha Yoga Center.

ISHA CENTERS

India

Isha Yoga Center,
Velliangiri Foothills,
Semmedu (P.O.)
Coimbatore – 641114,
India.

Telephone: +91-422-2515345
Email: info@ishafoundation.org

United States

Isha Institute of Inner Sciences,
951 Isha Lane,
McMinnville, TN 37110,
USA.

Telephone: +1-931-668-1900
Email: usa@ishafoundation.org

United Kingdom

Isha Institute of Inner Sciences,
PO Box 559,
Isleworth TW7 5WR,
United Kingdom.

Telephone: +44-79 56 99 87 29
Email: uk@ishafoundation.org

Australia

Isha Foundation Australia,
Suite 1.5,
173 Lennox Street,
Richmond VIC 3121,
Melbourne.

Telephone: +61 433 643 215
Email: australia@ishafoundation.org

Singapore

Isha Singapore,
Block 805 05-636,
Chai Chee Road,
Singapore 460805.

Telephone: +65 96660197
Email: singapore@ishafoundation.org

Malaysia

Telephone: +60 17-366-5252
Email: malaysia@ishafoundation.org

Middle East

Telephone: +961-3-789-046, +961-3-747-178
Email: lebanon@ishafoundation.org

Sadhguru

ABOUT THE AUTHOR

Yogi, mystic, and visionary, Sadhguru is a spiritual master with a difference. An arresting blend of profundity and pragmatism, his life and work serve as a reminder that yoga is not an esoteric discipline from an outdated past, but a contemporary science, vitally relevant to our times. Probing, passionate and provocative, insightful, logical and unfailingly witty, Sadhguru's talks have earned him the reputation of a speaker and opinion-maker of international renown.

With speaking engagements that take him around the world, he is widely sought after by prestigious global forums to address issues as diverse as human rights, business values, and social, environmental and existential issues. He has been a delegate to the United Nations Millennium World Peace Summit, a member of the World Council of Religious and Spiritual Leaders and Alliance for New Humanity, a special invitee to the Australian

Leadership Retreat, Tallberg Forum, Indian Economic Summit 2005-2008, as well as a regular at the World Economic Forum in Davos. He was awarded the Indira Gandhi Paryavaran Puraskar (IGPP) for the year 2008 for Isha Foundation's Project GreenHands' efforts.

With a celebratory engagement with life on all levels, Sadhguru's areas of active involvement encompass fields as diverse as architecture and visual design, poetry and painting, ecology and horticulture, sports and music. He is the author and designer of several unique buildings and consecrated spaces at the Isha Yoga Center, which have wide attention for their combination of intense sacred power with strikingly innovative eco-friendly aesthetics.

Listeners have been ubiquitously impressed by his astute and incisive grasp of current issues and world affairs, as well as his unerringly scientific approach to the question of human wellbeing. Sadhguru is also the founder of Isha Foundation, a non-profit organization dedicated to the wellbeing of the individual and the world for the past three decades. Isha Foundation does not promote any particular ideology, religion, or race, but transmits inner sciences of universal appeal.

www.sadhguru.org